NEVADA

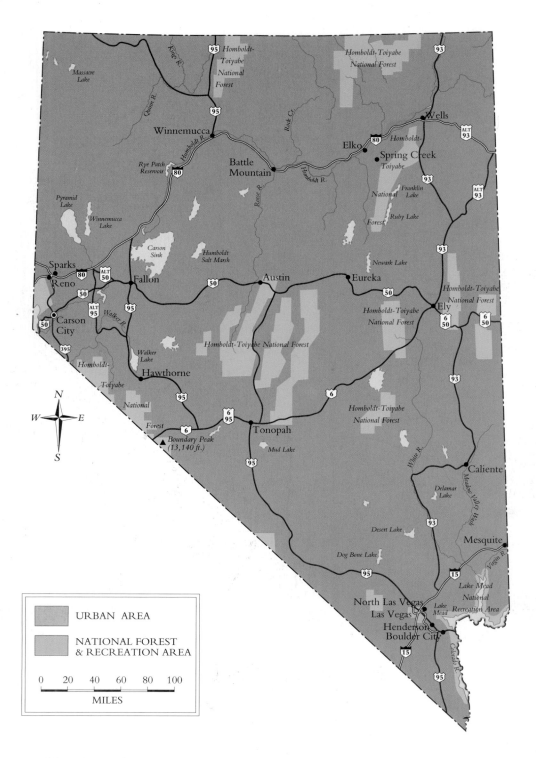

Massacre
Lake

Kings R.

Quinn R.

95

Humboldt-
Toiyabe
National
Forest

95

Rock Cr.

Humboldt-Toiyabe
National Forest

93

Wells

95

Winnemucca

Humboldt R.

Battle
Mountain

Elko

80

ALT
93

Humboldt-

Rye Patch
Reservoir

80

Reese R.

Humboldt R.

Spring Creek

Toiyabe

93

Pyramid
Lake

Franklin
Lake

ALT
93

National

Winnemucca
Lake

Carson
Sink

Humboldt
Salt Marsh

Forest

Ruby Lake

93

Sparks

80

ALT
50

Reno

50

Fallon

50

Austin

Newark Lake

Eureka

Humboldt-Toiyabe
National Forest

50

Ely

Humboldt-Toiyabe
National Forest

6
50

6
50

ALT
95

Walker R.

95

Carson
City

50

395

Walker
Lake

Humboldt-Toiyabe National Forest

6

93

Homboldt-

Toiyabe

Hawthorne

95

National

6

Forest

Boundary Peak
(13,140 ft.)

95

6
95

Tonopah

Humboldt-Toiyabe
National Forest

White R.

Caliente

Meadow Valley Wash

95

Mud Lake

Delamar
Lake

N
W   E
S

Desert Lake

93

Mesquite

Dog Bone Lake

95

15

Virgin R.

North Las Vegas

Lake
Mead

Lake Mead
National

Las Vegas

Recreation Area

Henderson
Boulder City

15

Colorado R.

95

URBAN AREA

NATIONAL FOREST
& RECREATION AREA

0   20   40   60   80   100

MILES

NEVADA BY ROAD

CELEBRATE THE STATES
NEVADA

Rebecca Stefoff

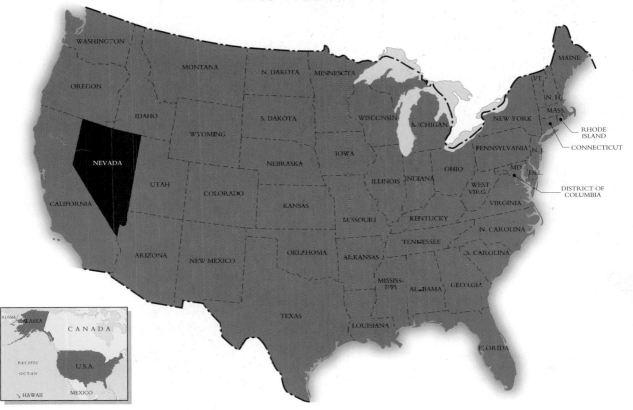

BENCHMARK BOOKS

MARSHALL CAVENDISH
NEW YORK

Benchmark Books
Marshall Cavendish Corporation
99 White Plains Road
Tarrytown, New York 10591-9001

Library of Congress Cataloging-in-Publication Data

Stefoff, Rebecca, 1951–
Nevada / Rebecca Stefoff.
p.   cm. — (Celebrate the states)
Includes bibliographical references and index.
ISBN 0-7614-1073-2
1. Nevada—Juvenile literature. [1. Nevada.] I. Title. II. Series.
F841.3 .S72 2001 979.3—dc21   00-057967

Maps and graphics supplied by Oxford Cartographers, Oxford, England

Photo research by Candlepants Incorporated

Cover photo: Larry Angier

The photographs in this book are used by permission and through the courtesy of; *Corbis*: 39; David Muench, 6-7, 10-11, 15, 22, 101, 122(top); Phil Schermeister, 13, 111, 119(lower); Richard Cummins, 20, 68-69,127; Kennen Ward, 24; Tim Thompson, 24-25; D. Boone, 28-29, 59; Schenectady Museum; Hall of Electrical History Foundation, 49; Bettmann,50, 129(left), 130, 131, 132, 133(top), 134(lower); Joseph Sohm; Chromosohm Inc., 52-53, 116; Roger Ressmeyer, 57; L. Clarke, 60; Dan Lamont, 64; Lois Ellen Frank, 66; James Marshall, 75; Morton Beebe, 80, 102; Galen Rowell, 82, 112, 137; Laurence Fordyce, 83; Tom Bean, 84, 98-99; Reuters News Media Inc., 92, 94; Ted Streshinsky, 96; Macduff Everton, 104; D. Robert Franz, 119(top); Annie Griffiths-Belt, 125. *Larry Angiers*:17, 27, 65, 72, 78, 86-87, 105, 108, 109, 115, back cover. *Caroline Fox,* 19. *CZ Harris*: 25. *Nevada Historical Society*: 30-31, 34, 37, 38, 40, 41, 46, 48, 89, 90, 129(right), 133(lower), 134(top), 135. *University of Nevada Press/John Ries*: 91. *Tom McHugh/ National Audubon Society/hoto Researchers Inc*: 122(lower).

Printed in Italy

3   5   6   4

CONTENTS

NEVADA IS . . .

Nevada is Las Vegas, a city built on gambling and famous for its nightlife and bright lights.

"Anyone in the whole country will tell you, *this* is the place to have fun! Everybody comes to Las Vegas sooner or later—rock groups, movie stars, boxers, wrestlers, swingers, kids, grandmas on charter buses. No matter what your game, Vegas is the ultimate playground."   —Dale Ewell, casino employee

"Las Vegas is a nightmare. It's the symbol of everything in our culture that is greedy, vulgar, cheap, and fake."
                  —Philosophy professor from California after visiting Nevada

But Nevada is also huge stretches of rugged, almost empty land.

"You know what we have a lot of here? Desert. It's more interesting than it sounds, though."   —Seventh-grade girl in Ely

"Here's what Nevada really is: not Las Vegas, not Reno, just miles and miles of road, up through a pass and down into the flatland over and over again, hardly any trees, only a few little towns, just land. Sometimes, when I'm driving at night, I'll pass hundreds of cattle on the road, maybe a few deer, and just two or three cars or trucks all night long. Sometimes when I'm passing through in the daytime I look at those mountains and think to myself that I'd like to get out of the truck and see what's behind them someday."
                          —R. J. Oates, long-haul trucker

Nevada has attracted many different kinds of settlers, from the stubbornly independent adventurers of the early days to the suburban homesteaders of the state's new land rush.

"Try to imagine what life was like here in pioneer days. The few people who came here had to do everything and make everything for themselves. It was like living on the moon. There's a book by Sarah Elizabeth Thompson Olds about her experiences home-steading in Nevada. The title says it all: *Twenty Miles from a Match.*"
—Mary Alstree, retired teacher, Reno

"Nevada today is a strange combination of a sophisticated society and a mining frontier; while there have been liberal attitudes toward gambling, divorce, and prostitution, powerful conservative elements dominate the state's politics."
—Nevada historian Russell R. Elliott

Native Americans have lived in Nevada for thousands of years, adapting their ways of life to the resources it offered. European explorers and American pioneers, however, saw Nevada as just a dry and dangerous obstacle to be crossed. Only when the land revealed its mineral riches did settlers come to Nevada. Things had changed a lot by the dawn of the twenty-first century, when Nevada was America's fastest-growing state. Although the population boom is shaping the state's economic and political future, the influences of the pioneer past and of the land itself remain strong.

1 SNOW, SAND, AND SAGEBRUSH

"This is the *real* West," a Nevada rancher declares proudly, one booted foot resting in the open door of his weathered pickup truck, as he gestures at a brown landscape under a brilliant sky, with low, rounded mountains on the horizon. The air carries a western tang—the mingled scents of sagebrush, dust, and, yes, a hint of cattle manure. The rancher looks around and adds, "It doesn't get any better than this."

Most of Nevada looks so much like the background to a western movie that you half expect to see a stagecoach clattering around a bend in the road, with masked gunslingers in hot pursuit. That probably won't happen, but if you spend much time in Nevada you are likely to see cowboys herding cattle, abandoned mining camps, and other Old West sights, set amid some of the most rugged geography in western North America.

THE GREAT BASIN

Nevada is shaped like a giant wedge driven between the Rocky Mountains and the Sierra Nevada, the California mountain range that rises across Nevada's western border. Nevada is bordered by Oregon and Idaho in the north, Utah in the east, Arizona in the southeast, and California in the west.

Like the Sierra Nevada, the state got its name from *nevada*, a

A desert campfire offers the promise of solitude, quiet, and starry skies. "I've had some great skywatching camping out in the middle of nowhere," says a member of an astronomy club in Reno.

Spanish word meaning "snow-covered." The name is a little misleading, however, for although Nevada does have some towering, snow-tipped peaks, the state consists mostly of dry semidesert and low, dusty mountain ranges. Its highest point is 13,143-foot Boundary Peak, which straddles the Nevada-California border. On the opposite side of the state, not far from the Utah border, stands Wheeler Peak, Nevada's second-highest mountain at 13,083 feet. Plenty of other peaks around the state rise above 10,000 feet.

Most of Nevada lies within a large geographic region that extends into Utah, Idaho, Oregon, and southern California. In the nineteenth century, explorer John Charles Frémont named this region the Great Basin because it is like an immense basin, or bowl, between the Rocky Mountain ranges and the Sierra Nevada, with all of its streams flowing inward rather than toward the sea. Nevada forms by far the largest portion of the Great Basin.

The Great Basin is made up of a hundred or more smaller basins or flatlands separated by rows of mountain ranges that run north-south. Geographer Clarence Dutton compared these ranges to "an army of caterpillars marching toward Mexico." Nearly all of Nevada is covered with these "caterpillar" ranges. The ranges are close together. As the road climbs to the crest of a pass through one range, you can gaze ahead to see it crossing the level basin below and then rising up to the next crest. In the summer, the landscape seems to shimmer with heat haze and dust.

Nevada's northeastern corner lies outside the Great Basin. This part of Nevada resembles the high, windswept plains of eastern Oregon and southern Idaho. The Bruneau, Jarbidge, and Owyhee Rivers rise in this part of the state and flow north. Nevada's south-eastern "point," a desert region of sand and sunbaked red rock, also falls outside the Great Basin. There, the Muddy and Virgin Rivers flow south into the Colorado River, which defines Nevada's border with Arizona and drains into the Gulf of California, an arm of the Pacific Ocean.

The state's four largest rivers, however, drain into the basin. The Truckee flows down from the Sierra Nevada into Pyramid Lake, near the state's western border. The Walker flows into Walker Lake, farther south. The Humboldt and Carson Rivers flow into sinks— marshy, low-lying depressions. Most of Nevada's smaller rivers and streams end in sinks or in playas, which are large stretches of dry, cracked clay. Some parts of the state, such as the Black Rock Desert in the northeastern corner, have huge playas. For miles, the earth looks like a giant jigsaw puzzle cut into pieces as much as a foot

Few roads cross the cracked, dry playa of the Black Rock Desert in Nevada's northwestern corner. Tabitha Brown, a pioneer who left the Oregon Trail for a "shortcut" in 1846, crossed the Black Rock and later recalled, "We had sixty miles of desert without grass or water."

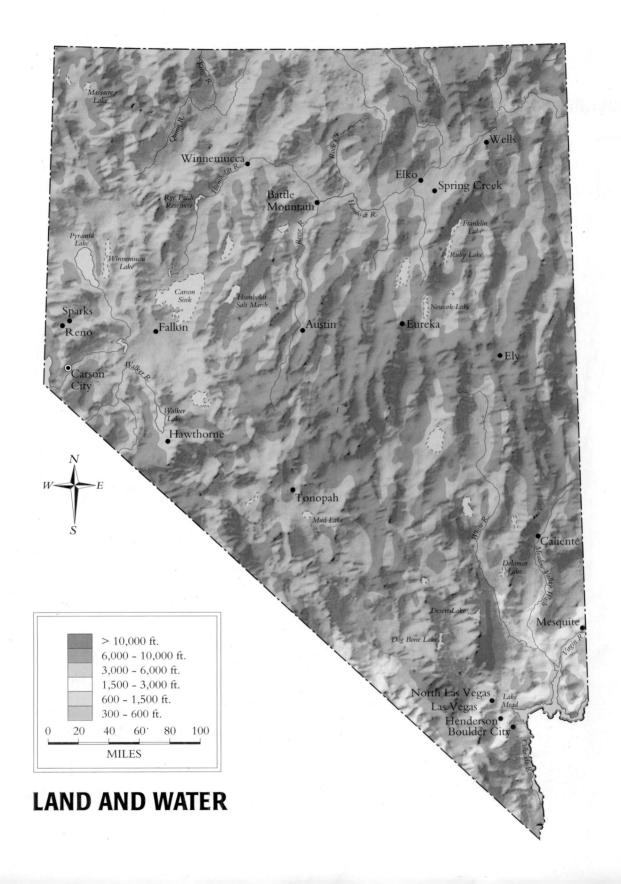

Massacre
Lake

Kings R.

Quinn R.

Wells

Winnemucca

Rock Cr.

Humboldt R.

Elko

Spring Creek

Rye Patch
Reservoir

Battle
Mountain

Humbodt R.

Franklin
Lake

Pyramid
Lake

Reese R.

Ruby Lake

Winnemucca
Lake

Carson
Sink

Humboldt
Salt Marsh

Newark Lake

Sparks

Fallon

Austin

Eureka

Reno

Ely

Carson
City

Walker R.

Walker
Lake

Hawthorne

Tonopah

Mud Lake

White R.

Caliente

Delamar
Lake

Meadow Valley Wash

Desert Lake

Mesquite

Dog Bone Lake

Virgin R.

North Las Vegas
Las Vegas

Lake
Mead

Henderson
Boulder City

Colorado R.

N
W   E
S

> 10,000 ft.
6,000 – 10,000 ft.
3,000 – 6,000 ft.
1,500 – 3,000 ft.
600 – 1,500 ft.
300 – 600 ft.

0   20   40   60   80   100

MILES

LAND AND WATER

MONSTERS FROM ANCIENT WATERS

Nevada wasn't always dry. During the last ice age, which ended about 11,000 years ago, its higher mountain ranges were covered with sheets of ice. Rivers draining from this ice formed large lakes. Lahontan, Nevada's largest ice-age lake, once covered 8,450 square miles of western Nevada. For thousands of years, though, Lake Lahontan has been drying up. All that remains today are Pyramid and Walker Lakes, Humboldt and Carson Sinks, dozens of playas, and the Black Rock, Smoke Creek, and Granite Creek Deserts, which used to be lake floor.

Before there were lakes, there was the sea. Millions of years ago, Nevada was covered by warm, shallow seas filled with life. The remains of plants and animals fell to the sea bottom, were covered with sand and mud, and over long ages became fossils. Among the creatures preserved beneath Nevada's ancient seas were ichthyosaurs, twenty-five-foot-long reptiles with large eyes, long snouts, and sharp teeth. Nevada has made this impressive hunter its official state fossil.

thick. Many of the state's waterways are seasonal. They flow freely in winter and spring but dry up completely by summer's end.

The largest natural lake in the state is Pyramid, named for an island that reminded explorer Frémont of the pyramids of Egypt. Lake Tahoe, a magnificent blue gem nestled in the foothills of the Sierra Nevada, is larger, but part of it lies in California. Largest of all is Lake Mead, an artificial reservoir created by the damming of the Colorado River.

HOT AND DRY

Nevada has a semidesert climate. Only patches of the state are true desert—bare rock or sand with few plants. In these deserts, precipitation—moisture that falls as rain or snow—may total less than five inches a year. Over the entire state, average yearly precipitation is seven inches, making Nevada the driest state in the nation. The higher mountains, which receive heavy snowfall, are the wettest parts of the state.

Nevada's storms can be fierce. Winter blizzards are rare, but occasionally they shut down highways and cut off mountain towns for days at a time. Even worse are the summer thunderstorms. These lightning-wracked downpours may last less than half an hour but wipe out roads, bridges—and, in some tragic cases, unlucky campers or hikers caught in canyons as flash floods roar down upon them.

Lake Tahoe, shared by Nevada and California, is the largest high-mountain lake in North America, with an area of almost two hundred square miles.

The southeastern Nevada desert rears up into wind-carved rock ramparts around Valley of Fire State Park.

The opposite of storm, of course, is sunshine, and Nevada has plenty of sunny days. "The sun is this place's most precious resource," says a retired accountant from Connecticut who moved to the outskirts of Las Vegas to enjoy cloudless skies on the golf course. He has many chances to enjoy that resource—Las Vegas has up to 320 sunny days a year.

But with that sun comes heat. In the summer, it's not unusual for Nevada to record the nation's highest temperatures, up to 120 degrees Fahrenheit in the southern tip of the state. Winter temperatures in the northern mountains have plummeted as low as -50 degrees Fahrenheit, recorded at San Jacinto in 1937.

Nevada is famous for large temperature shifts during a single day. Especially in late spring and early fall, daytime highs and lows may be fifty degrees apart. People who sweltered in shorts and T-shirts all afternoon may find themselves shivering in sweaters as soon as the sun goes down.

WILD THINGS

The hardy, aromatic, gray-green shrub called sagebrush is Nevada's state flower, and for good reason. Sagebrush flourishes in semidesert conditions and covers a fifth of the state. In the south, creosote and mesquite bushes are common. Yucca plants, which produce white flowers on spikes, grow in the warmer parts of the state, as do their larger and shaggier cousins, Joshua trees. Nevada has more than two dozen kinds of cactus, some of which produce surprisingly colorful and delicate blossoms among their spines.

Large expanses of Nevada are treeless, except where home owners have planted shade trees or decorative palm trees. Forest covers only about 12 percent of the state. Piñon and juniper trees carpet the lower mountain slopes. Higher up, pines and firs flourish. High forests in the southern half of the state may also include bristlecone

A bristlecone pine in Great Basin National Park. Sadly, park officials must keep the locations of the oldest trees secret to protect these ancient treasures from vandalism.

pines. These tough, low-growing trees are among the world's longest-living plants—some are thousands of years old. Throughout the state, streams are bordered by tangles of chokecherry, alder, willow, and cottonwood trees whose leaves turn vivid yellow in the fall.

Dozens of species of birds make their home in Nevada—or pass through it. Hundreds of thousands of ducks and geese stop in western Nevada's lakes and streams while migrating. So do pelicans. You may associate these big-billed birds with ocean beaches and harbors, but the American white pelican breeds on the islands of Pyramid Lake. Golden and bald eagles, owls, falcons, and songbirds like the mountain bluebird also make their home in the state.

The mule deer is the most common large wild animal in Nevada, but the state also has herds of bighorn sheep, pronghorn antelope, and elk. Nevada also has the nation's largest population of wild burros and mustangs. These animals are the descendants of horses and donkeys introduced to the Americas by the Spaniards in the sixteenth century. Animals that ran away or were abandoned adapted to life in the wilderness. Now, generations later, they are wild. Many visitors to Nevada are thrilled to catch a glimpse of a mustang galloping across the plain with its mane streaming in the wind, but some folks have greater admiration for the tough, sturdy burros. "These little burros may not look as romantic as wild horses," says a ranger at Nevada's Red Rock Canyon National Conservation Area, "but they are smart, nimble, very efficient grazers. They are supremely well adapted to life in this environment." If you drive along the back roads of southern Nevada, look for light-colored patches about knee-high in the fields. Those patches are the pale muzzles of burros, who will raise their heads, ears erect, to watch you pass.

"The wild horse in action is a beautiful sight," wrote Hope Ryden, a filmmaker who fought to save the mustangs of Nevada and the West.

American white pelicans on Pyramid Lake. Flocks of these birds breed on inland waters throughout western North America in spring and summer, then spend the winters in warmer coastal waters farther south.

Descendants of escaped livestock from as long ago as the 1500s, wild burros flourish in sagebrush country, sometimes picking their patient, surefooted way along narrow trails or down steep gorges in search of food or water.

SAVING THE ENDANGERED CUI-UI

The cui-ui (pronounced "kwee-wee") is a slow, two-foot-long fish that lives in Nevada's Pyramid Lake and nowhere else in the world. Cui-ui spend most of the year drifting along the lake bottom, feeding on the tiny creatures that live there. Between April and June, however, they swim upstream into the Truckee River to breed.

Once the cui-ui was a staple food of the Paiute Indians, who caught the fish along the Truckee. But in the twentieth century, as water was drained from the Truckee to supply farms and towns, the river's level fell. As less fresh water entered Pyramid Lake, the mineral content of the lake changed, threatening the cui-ui's health. In addition, the river was no longer strong enough to wash away the sand at its mouth, so a large sandbar built up. The sandbar kept the cui-ui from swimming upriver to breed. The future of the cui-ui looked dim.

Then, in 1973, the Pyramid Lake Paiute Tribe established a hatchery, a place where adult cui-ui are brought to discharge their eggs. When they hatch, the young fish are placed in tanks until they are large enough to be safely released into Pyramid Lake. The work at the hatchery, combined with efforts to remove the sandbar and maintain water flow in the Truckee, may help the cui-ui recover so that this rare and ancient fish will survive in its only home.

Smaller kinds of wildlife abound in Nevada. Rabbits are most common, but there are also badger, red fox, coyote, mink, muskrat, beaver, raccoon, and porcupine. Like other hot, dry, rocky places, Nevada has an abundance of reptiles, including the big, slow-moving desert tortoise, the state reptile. Snakes include rattlers, garters, and gopher snakes. The state is home to several dozen kinds of lizards. They may look like small dinosaurs, but these shy creatures are harmless—except for the black-and-orange Gila monster, whose bite is mildly poisonous but who would much rather avoid you than bite you.

WHERE THE PEOPLE ARE

For a long time, Nevada was one of the nation's most thinly settled states. But that is changing fast. In 1980 Nevada ranked

The desert tortoise, Nevada's state reptile, is too slow to escape predators—or collectors. Tortoise populations are suffering because people are taking them as pets.

forty-third out of the fifty states in population. By 1998 it had moved up to thirty-sixth. During the 1990s its population increased by more than 50 percent—the highest rate of increase in the country.

The vast majority of Nevadans live in the urban areas around Las Vegas and Reno. Outside the cities, people are spread sparsely across the landscape. The federal government owns 85 percent of Nevada, in the form of national forests, wildlife refuges, one national park,

Neon lights compete with a flaming sunset as night falls over Las Vegas, the fastest-growing city in the United States.

Indian reservations, military sites such as the enormous Nellis Air Force Range, and vast tracts administered by the Bureau of Land Management (BLM). These lands have many uses—for example, ranchers graze livestock on BLM lands, and timber companies harvest trees from national forests—but they do not contain large towns. However, some Nevadans predict that if the state's population continues to skyrocket, there will be increasing pressure for development of land that now lies quiet and empty under the desert sky.

2 THE HEART OF THE GOLDEN WEST

Humboldt Lake, by Edwin Deakin

Nevada's state song ends: "Right in the heart of the golden west/Home means Nevada to me." Nevada has been golden in various ways. To its first inhabitants, it was a sun-bathed landscape painted in earthen colors. Later, Nevada drew prospectors with the lure of buried gold and silver. Today, the state's golden allure includes neon lights and big dreams of casino winnings.

PREHISTORIC PEOPLE

Scientists believe that the first Americans came from Asia thousands of years ago, during the ice age, when ocean levels were lower and a land bridge linked Siberia in northeastern Asia to Alaska. In time the descendants of these migrants spread out across the Americas. By 12,000 years ago, hunting people called Paleo-Indians were living in Nevada. Some Paleo-Indians lived in caves along Lake Lahontan, where stone dart points, fishing nets, and baskets have been found. Elsewhere in Nevada, scientists have found stone spear points that Paleo-Indians used to bring down mammoths—huge, shaggy, elephant-like creatures that are now extinct.

Over the centuries, the weather grew drier and hotter. Big game became scarce, and people began hunting smaller prey such as tortoises, rabbits, and squirrels.

Around 300 B.C. the Anasazi culture appeared in Moapa Valley in southeastern Nevada. At first they lived in pits roofed with sticks and mud, but by about A.D. 700 they had begun building above-ground structures of sun-dried clay brick. The main Anasazi community, home to between 10,000 and 20,000 people, consisted of pit houses, caves, and large brick structures called pueblos, some with as many as a hundred rooms. The Anasazi were also master potters and farmers. Sometime after 1150 the Anasazi disappeared from Nevada. Scientists think that drought or warfare may have driven them east to Arizona and New Mexico. In the 1920s their abandoned city was rediscovered and named Pueblo Grande de Nevada. Today it is more often called the Lost City. After Hoover Dam was built to harness the waters of the Colorado River, the rising waters of Lake Mead covered the city.

NATIVE AMERICANS

Other Native American peoples flourished in Nevada after the Anasazi left. The four major groups were the Northern Paiutes in the western part of the state, the Shoshones in eastern and central Nevada, the Southern Paiutes in the southeastern corner, and the Washos around Lake Tahoe.

The Indians gathered wild foods such as pine nuts, raspberries, wild carrots, and seeds that they pounded into a flour to thicken their soups. In the mountains they hunted antelopes and bighorn sheep. Lower down they took rabbits and other small game. The Indians used clever traps to capture animals. Wooden or stuffed decoys lured waterfowl to ponds where they could be taken with nets or spears. Insects such as grasshoppers were also a valued food.

A member of the Northern Paiute group of Native Americans, whose homeland is in western Nevada and parts of Idaho and Oregon.

Nevada's Indians traveled from place to place with the seasons, moving from one food source to another. They usually wintered in sheltered valleys, where they built snug pit houses. During the rest of the year they lived in shelters of grass or reed laid across pole frameworks. They wore clothing of deerskin or pounded sagebrush bark. Rabbit skin blankets were prized possessions.

The Indians usually lived in small bands, but they would gather

HOW THE MOTH CAUGHT FIRE IN HIS WINGS

The Paiutes have many traditional legends that tell how things came to be the way they are. This story describes the origin of the red-winged moth.

A wicked magician named Un-nu-pit loved fire so much that he slept on hot coals. Un-nu-pit made all the trouble in the world.

Un-nu-pit had many warriors and dancers who went out into the world to do his bidding. One of them was named Ne-ab. One night Ne-ab flew to a Paiute camp. Fluttering his black wings like a bat, he danced in and out of the Paiutes' firelight, teasing the young people and trying to make them chase him so that they would run into the fire. But Ne-ab was overcome by the beautiful eyes of the young maidens around the fire, and he fell into the flames, which scorched and killed him.

Then Un-nu-pit raised up Ne-ab, wrapped him in a silky soft blanket, and hid him safely away all through the long winter. The following spring, the maidens in the Paiute camp remembered the dancer who had once visited them. They missed his antics. Then a winged being fluttered into the fire-light. In was Ne-ab, but he was no longer black. His body and wings were velvety gray, like the ashes of an old fire, but the underside of his wings glowed like flame as he danced before the maidens.

in larger groups for rabbit hunts or pine-nut harvests. These would be times of celebration, with dancing, games, and gambling—which existed in Nevada long before the first casino was built.

PASSING THROUGH

After Spain conquered Mexico in the early sixteenth century, the Spaniards claimed a large territory north of Mexico, from Texas to California. For several hundred years, however, Spain showed no interest in Nevada. Not until 1776 did someone from Spanish Mexico enter Nevada. While looking for a route from Santa Fe, New Mexico, to Monterey, California, Father Francisco Garcés possibly passed through Nevada's southern tip. After that first visit, Spain and Mexico again left Nevada alone. In the 1840s, after the Mexican War, the United States gained ownership of Nevada. But even before that time a number of American and British adventurers were active in Nevada.

The first to appear were the fur trappers and traders, sometimes called mountain men. They were looking for beaver, whose smooth, waterproof fur was in great demand for hats and coats. Two of the most widely traveled mountain men were Peter Skene Ogden, who worked for the British, and Jedediah Smith, an American. In the 1820s Ogden trapped and explored in northeastern Nevada, along the Humboldt River, and around Walker Lake. Smith arrived in Nevada in 1826, leading a band of trappers from Utah. They crossed the southern tip of Nevada to California and then returned eastward, heading across central Nevada and suffering dreadful hardships in the waterless Great Basin. Smith is believed to be the first white person to cross Nevada. He was the first to report the conditions deep inside the Great Basin.

Beginning in the 1840s, thousands of Americans migrated west along the wagon route called the Oregon and California Trail. Those bound for the Pacific Northwest did not usually enter Nevada, but many of those bound for California crossed Nevada, reaching California through passes in the Sierra Nevada. To these early travelers, Nevada was just an obstacle, something to get through on the way to something better. This was even more true after gold was discovered in California in 1848. Americans passed through Nevada, cursing its dust and heat, on their way to the California goldfields. Within a few years, however, Nevada would become a destination in its own right.

THE COMSTOCK LODE

In 1850, Congress created the Utah Territory, which included much of present-day Nevada. The Mormons, a religious group who

Peter Skene Ogden, working for the British, tried to outexplore and out-trap the American mountain men. In 1828 he discovered the Humboldt River, which he named the Unknown River. Ogden followed the Humboldt to its swampy sink, finding that it did not lead westward to the Pacific Ocean as he at first hoped.

had settled Utah, founded a few settlements in the Carson Valley. They even found small amounts of gold east of Lake Tahoe.

In 1859, miners struck gold there, at a place they called Gold Hill. A few months later a pair of prospectors made a startling discovery nearby. Seeing gold flecks in the sand of a spring, they dug deeper and found a ledge of solid gold. A third miner, Henry Paige Comstock, immediately claimed that he owned the land. Although everyone in the area regarded Comstock as lazy and untrustworthy, he managed to get a share of the claim.

The gold ledge was part of an enormous vein of precious metal

Henry Paige Comstock did not discover the rich Comstock Lode. Instead, he convinced its finders that he had a claim to the land. Locally regarded as lazy and "half-mad," Comstock not only profited from the discovery but left his name embedded in history.

After the discovery of the Comstock Lode, buildings sprouted on the region's once barren hills.

running through the hills. This fabulous treasure, soon known as the Comstock Lode, kicked off a new gold rush. At first, no one realized just how large the Comstock was. Nor did they recognize what it held. But after miners complained about the blue clay that was constantly in their way, experts discovered that the clay was silver ore, and that the Comstock Lode was even richer in silver than in gold. A California paper published the news, and the rush was on.

During Nevada's mining boom years, towns such as Treasure City blossomed briefly and then faded.

Tent camps called Gold Hill and Silver City sprang up as miners rushed across the Sierra Nevada to the region they had passed through so impatiently just a few years before. The biggest community was named Virginia City. The winter of 1859–1860 was a bitter time on the Comstock. Most miners did not bring enough food with them, and farms and ranches were scarce in the region. Once snow had closed the Sierra Nevada passes, it was almost impossible to bring supplies from California. Those who had supplies could sell them for astonishing prices—sacks of flour went for $885 each. As in other gold rushes, most of the people who made fortunes were not the hopeful miners but the enterprising men and women who provided them with goods and entertainment.

STATEHOOD

The inrush of people to Virginia City and the mines of western Nevada led to lawlessness, confusion, and fights over mining claims. The Utah officials, far away in Salt Lake City, had a hard time governing their wild frontier territory.

Virginia City miners in 1860. Mining was dangerous work. One observer wrote, "To describe in detail the manifold ways in which men have lost their lives in these mines would be a needless catalogue of horrors."

Trouble also arose with the Native Americans, who resented the Comstockers for killing all the game and cutting down the trees that produced pine nuts, a staple of the Indian diet. Although the Paiute leader Winnemucca urged the Indians to remain peaceful, fighting broke out after white men kidnapped two Paiute girls in the spring of 1860. The arrival of U.S. Army troops ended the so-called Pyramid Lake War.

In 1861 Congress took western Nevada away from Utah, naming it the Nevada Territory. Carson City, a town that had grown on the site of a pioneer trading post, was made Nevada's capital. Later in the 1860s, Congress would give Nevada additional territory from Utah and Arizona, creating the state's present boundaries.

The Comstock brought overnight growth to western Nevada. By 1863 Virginia City had grown from a huddle of tents reached only by a burro track into the second most important town in the American West, after San Francisco. Lying at the center of a network of roads, it had an opera house, four banks, six churches—and 110 saloons and gambling halls.

The rising conflict over slavery in the United States led to the outbreak of the Civil War in 1861. The Nevada Territory supported the Northern or Union side, and wealth from the Comstock helped pay for the Union war effort. President Abraham Lincoln was eager to make Nevada a state, partly as a reward for its loyalty and partly because doing so would add another "free" state to the Senate vote on ending slavery. He officially named Nevada the country's thirty-sixth state on October 31, 1864. Nevada's first congressman and senators rushed to Washington, D.C., to cast vital votes for the Thirteenth Amendment, which abolished slavery. Less than six months later, when word of Lincoln's assassination reached Nevada, the streets of Virginia City were draped in black, the church bells tolled, and even the saloons closed for a day.

BOOM AND BUST

The hills around Virginia City were honeycombed with caverns and tunnels where men labored day and night, often in scorching heat, to claw the precious ore from its resting place. Conditions were very dangerous, even after an engineer named Philip Deidesheimer invented a method of joining timbers into hollow cubes to reinforce the tunnels on all sides. Like many others on the Comstock, Deidesheimer failed to make a fortune—he missed the chance to patent his invention, which was immediately adopted at all the mines.

The new method of shoring up the mines, combined with the constant construction of new buildings, created a ravenous appetite for timber, which had to be brought to the treeless Comstock from the slopes of the Sierra Nevada, ten or more miles away. Hauling the logs in wagons was expensive and time-consuming, so in 1867 loggers began using flumes to move timber to the mines. A flume was a shallow trough of wooden planks, partly filled with water from a mountain stream. Logs loaded into flumes in the mountains floated down over canyons and around hills to lumberyards far below. In 1875 a new fifteen-mile flume was built. The first things to travel down it were not logs but two little boats carrying lumber company officials and a reporter. The reporter later described the bone-rattling, terrifying ride: "You have nothing to hold to; you have

"IN RAWHIDE"

You'll have a hard time finding the ghost town of Rawhide on the map today, but when this song was published in 1908, Rawhide was a gold boomtown. During the glory years of 1907 and 1908, an estimated 10,000 people swarmed into Mineral County. Most of the town was destroyed by a fire that raced through the tents and wooden buildings on September 4, 1908.

Words By Fred Jones   **Music By Glenn W. Ashley**

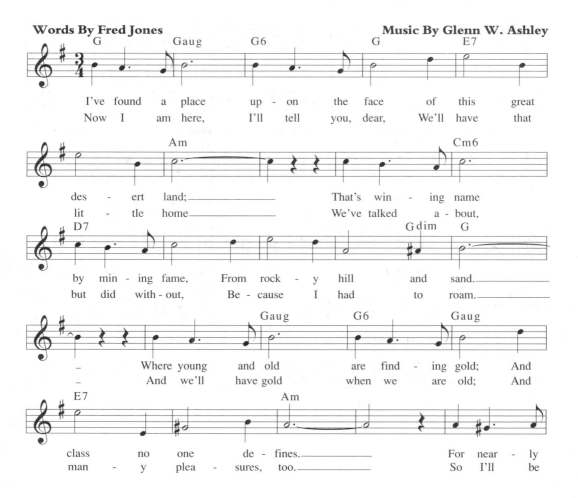

I've found a place up-on the face of this great
Now I am here, I'll tell you, dear, We'll have that

des-ert land;_____ That's win-ing name
lit-tle home_____ We've talked a-bout,

by min-ing fame, From rock-y hill and sand._____
but did with-out, Be-cause I had to roam._____

— Where young and old are find-ing gold; And
— And we'll have gold when we are old; And

class no one de-fines._____ For near-ly
man-y plea-sures, too._____ So I'll be

A flume in Clear Creek Canyon in 1890, one of many waterways that carried logs from the Sierra Nevada slopes to the treeless mining districts.

only to sit still, take all the water that comes—drenching you like a plunge through the surf—and wait for eternity." Today, similar rides—although shorter and safer—are a popular feature at water parks.

In addition to statehood, the 1860s brought a revolution in transportation. The first railway across the West, completed in 1869, ran through north-central Nevada along the route once followed by wagon trains. Other, shorter lines followed, serving the mining region and linking it with other parts of the state. Towns such as Reno and Elko sprang up along the railroads.

Still, the Comstock Lode dominated Nevada's growth and its economy. But the twenty-year boom, one of the richest in mining history, was followed by one of the biggest busts. By 1880 almost all the gold and silver had been stripped from the Comstock. Mining booms elsewhere in Nevada also went bust around the same time. People drifted away, and many of the rich, rowdy mining communities became ghost towns, empty wind-worn shells that gathered dust and tumbleweeds as they slowly crumbled. From a high of 62,000 in 1880, Nevada's population fell to around 42,000 in 1900.

The whole cycle started again in 1900, when a prospector hunting for his lost burro discovered silver in southwestern Nevada and established the mining town of Tonopah. Soon other miners struck gold nearby. The tiny town of Las Vegas was founded in the southern part of the state as a hub for railway lines to the new boomtowns. Within a few years, these mines had declined, but by then, Nevada was entering a new era.

MODERN NEVADA

As early as the 1850s, people began raising cattle and sheep in Nevada. Some were Mormon settlers who brought livestock from Utah. Others were California ranchers who wanted to take advantage of the growing market in the mining region. As the mining booms fizzled, some miners turned to ranching. The railroads helped, giving ranchers a way to get their livestock to market. But like mining, ranching had its ups and downs. An economic depression in the 1890s hurt many ranchers, but World War I

(1914–1918) created greater demand for livestock, as nations bought huge quantities of food for their armies.

A severe depression struck in 1929, eventually plunging the whole country into a dark cloud of unemployment and poverty. To improve their state's economy, Nevadans made gambling legal in 1931. They also passed a law that made it easier for married couples to obtain divorces in Nevada than anywhere else in the United States. State legislators believed that people would come to Nevada to gamble and get divorced, and that while in Nevada they would spend money in hotels, restaurants, and shops as well as in casinos. Although the divorce law later lost its importance as such laws became more liberal in other states, the gambling law laid the foundation for what eventually became Nevada's number-

Raising sheep has been an important industry in Nevada since the late nineteenth century.

During the Great Depression, the construction of what is now called Hoover Dam provided work for thousands of people.

one industry. As soon as it passed, Californians streamed across the Sierra Nevada to Reno's first casinos.

The federal government fought the depression with public works projects that employed thousands of people. One of the largest was the construction of Boulder Dam (now called Hoover Dam) in a narrow canyon of the Colorado River southeast of Las Vegas. A new community, Boulder City, was founded to house the dam workers. Both it and Las Vegas grew during the five-year construction project, which ended in 1936. The dam controlled flooding on the river, stored water for irrigation, and provided electricity by harnessing the power of water flowing through great wheels called turbines.

World War II brought the world into the nuclear age when the United States dropped two atomic bombs on Japan to end the war in 1945. Although the atomic bomb was developed at a laboratory in New Mexico, after the war a large area of Nevada land was set

An atomic bomb is tested in the Nevada desert in 1951.

aside as a test site for nuclear weapons. Such weapons are still tested there, although all tests have been conducted underground since 1963.

Nevada enjoyed a new boom after the war's end—a boom in tourism. In 1946 a New York gangster named Benjamin "Bugsy" Siegel opened a casino-hotel called the Flamingo, beginning Las Vegas's transformation from just another desert town into a bustling, neon-lit place that some called Sin City and others called the Entertainment Capital of the World.

Nevada's population has grown a lot since 1970, largely due to its gambling and entertainment industries. The growth has been concentrated in the Reno and Las Vegas areas. These urban centers have had to deal with urban problems, including traffic congestion, air pollution, rising crime rates, and crowded schools. Water shortages are an especially challenging problem in a desert state that suffers from frequent droughts.

While many Nevadans are thrilled with their state's current boom, they also recognize the need to plan and control growth. "This state's full of ghost towns," says an elderly man who has spent his entire life in southern Nevada. "We need to learn some lessons from the past. Don't build too high, too fast, because if the bottom ever falls out, you're in trouble for sure." Then he adds, "Still, people are never going to give up their fun. Vegas won't become another ghost town."

3 HOW NEVADA WORKS

The state capitol in Carson City

The Silver State, as Nevada is called, is still governed from Carson City, a city of 41,000 nestled below the tree-covered slopes of the Sierra Nevada. The dome of the capitol building is sheathed in silver that flashes brilliantly in the Nevada sunshine—a fitting tribute to the state's first source of prosperity.

INSIDE GOVERNMENT

Nevada's state government is modeled on the federal government, which has three branches that enforce, make, and interpret the laws.

Executive. The executive branch of government is responsible for seeing that the state's laws are enforced. The six top executive branch officials are elected to four-year terms. The chief official is the governor, who oversees dozens of state boards, agencies, and departments concerned with education, environmental protection, economic development, health, and more. The lieutenant governor stands ready to substitute for the governor if needed and serves as president of the state senate.

The secretary of state supervises Nevada's business affairs, such as overseeing voter registration and the issuing of business licenses. The attorney general is the state's top lawyer, charged with representing Nevada in lawsuits and other legal matters. The treasurer

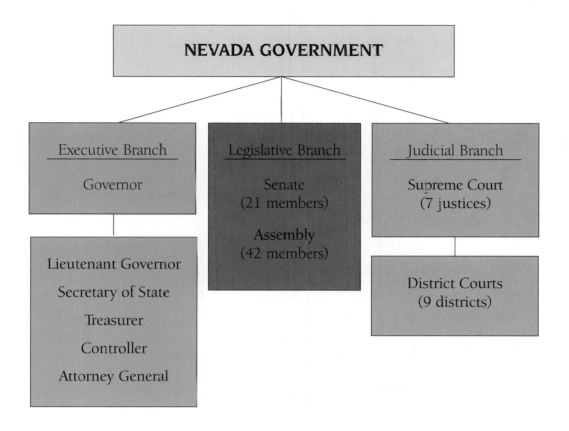

NEVADA GOVERNMENT

Executive Branch

Governor

Lieutenant Governor
Secretary of State
Treasurer
Controller
Attorney General

Legislative Branch

Senate
(21 members)

Assembly
(42 members)

Judicial Branch

Supreme Court
(7 justices)

District Courts
(9 districts)

manages the financial activities of state and local government, while the controller oversees the accounting systems that track such activities.

Legislative. The legislative branch of state government consists of two houses, the senate and the assembly. Voters elect twenty-one state senators to four-year terms and forty-two assembly members to two-year terms. These legislators make new laws and change existing ones. After both the senate and the assembly approve a proposal for a new law, called a bill, it goes to the governor. The governor either signs the bill, making it a law, or vetoes it, refusing to sign. A bill vetoed by the governor can still become law if two-thirds of both houses approve it again.

Judicial. The judicial branch consists of the court system, which is responsible for interpreting the law. On the bottom rung of the judicial ladder are municipal, small-claims, and local justice courts, where minor cases are heard. More serious cases go to the nine district courts. These courts also hear appeals from the lower courts, when one party in a case, dissatisfied with the lower court's decision, asks that the case be reviewed.

Nevada's highest court is its supreme court, which consists of seven justices elected to six-year terms. They review cases appealed from the district courts, and their chief responsibility is to determine whether those cases were properly tried under the laws set forth in Nevada's constitution.

SHOWDOWN AT YUCCA MOUNTAIN

At the beginning of the twenty-first century, no political issue in Nevada is hotter than the controversy over Yucca Mountain, where the federal government wants to store the nation's radioactive waste.

The U.S. Department of Energy (DOE) oversees the nuclear power plants, weapons labs, and research facilities that use radioactive material such as uranium and plutonium. Contaminated, radioactive waste—which is highly poisonous to living things—is piling up at those sites, and DOE officials believe that it is vital to move the waste to a single storage site where it can be monitored. The DOE is considering storing the nuclear waste at Yucca Mountain, about a hundred miles northwest of Las Vegas, on the federally owned Nellis Air Force Range. They want to build a network of tunnels one

Yucca Mountain's landscape may look empty and untroubled, but it is the site of a fierce battle over the disposal of the nation's radioactive waste.

thousand feet below Yucca Mountain's surface in which to store 77,000 tons of radioactive waste in thick, rustproof containers.

"It's an outrage," says Jerry Buswell of Las Vegas, echoing the estimated 70 percent of Nevadans who oppose the Yucca Mountain Project (YMP). "They've already blasted this state with nuclear testing, and now they want to make our home the dumping-ground for everybody's poison." Yet some Nevadans support the project, which could bring jobs for construction, technical, and security workers.

Many people oppose the YMP because of Yucca Mountain's history of volcanic and earthquake activity. The DOE cannot guarantee that earth movements will never cause radioactive leaks, contamination of the ground water, or even explosions at the storage facility. The danger is not merely an immediate one. Nuclear waste remains radioactive for a very long time—spent nuclear fuel remains dangerous for tens of thousands of years.

The DOE, however, believes the site is safe and is hoping to get the go-ahead to start construction soon. "Whatever happens, this fight is not over," says one anti-YMP activist. "If they really try to start construction, we'll bring in thousands of protestors, every day for years if we have to. The feds have no right to ram this down our throats—let them keep the nuclear waste in Washington, with all the hot air!"

NEVADA'S NUMBER-ONE INDUSTRY

The tourism, entertainment, and gambling industry directly or indirectly employs more than half of all working Nevadans. Nearly everyone who visits Nevada gambles—not just in Las Vegas and Reno but in small towns across the state. Casino communities such as Jackpot on the Idaho border, West Wendover on the Utah border, and Laughlin in the south near the California and Arizona borders let travelers gamble as soon as they enter Nevada. You don't even have to go into a casino: "The gas stations, drugstores, and laundromats in Nevada all have slot machines," one visitor from Oregon marveled. The taxes on gambling establishments contribute greatly to Nevada's treasury, while the lure of casinos leads out-of-state visitors to spend money on restaurants, hotels, and other activities. Each year, Las Vegas alone hosts more than 33 million such visitors.

Gambling has a long and checkered history in Nevada. Miners on the Comstock wagered and sometimes fought over high-stakes card games. Early gambling halls in the Reno-Tahoe area became the state's first casinos. In 1910, Nevada passed a law against

Slot machines were called "one-armed bandits" in the days when a gambler played by pulling a long lever at the machine's side. Today many slots operate by push button. "Makes it easier than ever to play them," commented one casino veteran on the change.

This casino's sign leaves no doubt that travelers have entered Nevada— and can now gamble.

gambling—but the practice didn't stop. Instead, gambling simply went underground. In 1931 Nevada made gambling legal once again. Phil Tobin, the state assemblyman who introduced the legalization, later said, "The state was practically broke but gambling wasn't contributing a cockeyed penny. I just wanted to see them

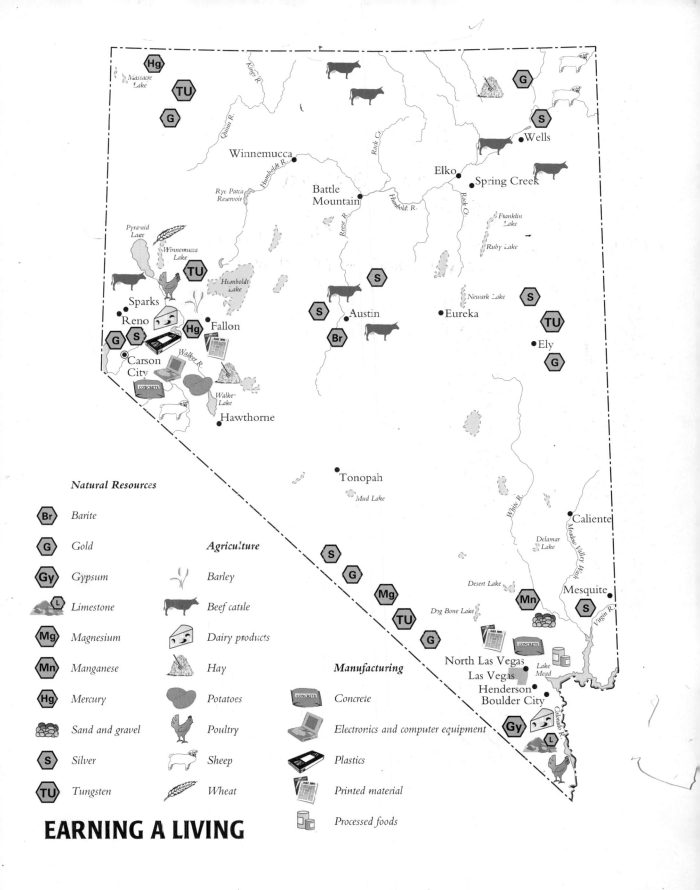

Massacre Lake

Kings R.

Quinn R.

Hg
TU
G

Winnemucca

Humboldt R.

Rye Patch Reservoir

Battle Mountain

Reese R.

Humboldt R.

Rock Cr.

Elko
Spring Creek

Rock Cr.

Wells

G
S

Franklin Lake

Ruby Lake

Pyramid Lake

Winnemucca Lake

TU

Humboldt Lake

Sparks
Reno

G S
Carson City

Hg
Fallon

Walker R.

S
Austin
Br

S
Eureka

Newark Lake

S

S
TU

Ely

G

Walker Lake
Hawthorne

Tonopah

Mud Lake

Caliente

Delamar Lake

Meadow Valley Wash

S
G
Mg
TU
G

Desert Lake

Dog Bone Lake

White R.

Mn

Mesquite

S

Virgin R.

North Las Vegas
Las Vegas
Henderson
Boulder City

Lake Mead

Colorado R.

Gy
L

Natural Resources

Br Barite

G Gold

Gy Gypsum

L Limestone

Mg Magnesium

Mn Manganese

Hg Mercury

Sand and gravel

S Silver

TU Tungsten

Agriculture

Barley

Beef cattle

Dairy products

Hay

Potatoes

Poultry

Sheep

Wheat

Manufacturing

Concrete

Electronics and computer equipment

Plastics

Printed material

Processed foods

EARNING A LIVING

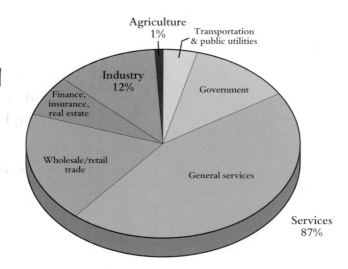

GROSS STATE PRODUCT: $59.7 BILLION

(2000 estimated)

Agriculture 1%

Transportation & public utilities

Industry 12%

Finance, insurance, real estate

Government

Wholesale/retail trade

General services

Services 87%

pay their way. That way, we could pick up money from the license fees." During the 1940s and 1950s organized crime gangs controlled many of Las Vegas's casinos. In the 1960s the state moved to clean up the gambling industry by forming a commission to oversee it and by allowing businesses to invest in casinos.

The 1990s brought yet another change to Nevada's gambling scene, particularly in Las Vegas. Hoping to shed the city's image of sin and shady associations, some casino and hotel owners began wooing families, providing rides, shows, game arcades, and shops geared to Middle American folks and their kids. Although gambling is still Las Vegas's main business, 12 percent of the city's visitors are under twenty-one. Late at night on the Strip, Vegas's casino-lined main boulevard, parents pushing strollers seem as numerous as stretch limos.

Despite the economic benefits of gambling, some Nevadans are worried about its importance in the state economy. Nevada has begun to recognize that compulsive gambling can lead to problems such as bankruptcy, family troubles, crime, and even suicide. Posters in some of the casinos list the warning signs of problem gambling or the phone number of Gamblers Anonymous, a self-help organization for people who cannot control their gambling.

One challenge to the mainstay of Nevada's economy is the growth of gambling in other states. When the Las Vegas casino industry began, gambling was legal only in Nevada and New Jersey. Now some form of gambling is legal in all but two states, and casinos owned by Native Americans have become top money earners in many parts of the country. Recognizing this problem, Las Vegas works hard to draw visitors by emphasizing its big-name entertainment and splashy architecture. One employee on the Strip explains it this way: "You can go to a casino on a reservation, or you can come to a whole city of casinos in Las Vegas."

LIVING OFF THE LAND

Aside from tourism, Nevada's key industries are generally based on the land. Mining has always been important to Nevada's economy. Copper was mined throughout the 1970s, but by 1980 demand had fallen and the state's large copper mines had closed. Today minerals such as gypsum, molybdenum, barite, limestone, and sand and gravel are big business. Gold is mined with new technologies that allow mining companies to remove tiny amounts of metal from the massive heaps of low-grade ore discarded during earlier gold rushes. Silver, opals, and turquoise are also mined.

Ranching remains Nevada's leading agricultural activity, with the

Traces of gold lurk in this black sand. Large corporations do most of the mining in Nevada, but a few solitary prospectors still probe the state's streams, deserts, and mountains. Some hope to hit it rich, others simply enjoy the activity.

largest cattle and sheep spreads in the northern half of the state. Nevada farmers, many of whom depend on water from irrigation projects to turn their dry ground into productive fields, grow alfalfa, oats, hay, and barley for livestock feed. They also raise potatoes, onions, wheat, and—where enough water is available—corn, tomatoes, and grapes. "The future of Nevada's agricultural development," points out historian Russell R. Elliott, "as it has always been, is tied to the problem of adequate water. Nevada's supply is as limited as the possible solutions to the problem." Many solutions focus on using the water supply more efficiently, such as covering irrigation canals to keep water from evaporating under the hot sun.

Livestock on the move during a cattle drive are forgiven for ignoring the yellow no-passing line on a state highway. Nevada's cattle industry dates from the 1850s, and the early herdsmen had to guide their livestock over much rougher terrain than this.

SILVER STATE BURGER

The restaurants and casinos of Las Vegas offer a dazzling variety of dishes from around the world. But if you want a real *Nevada* dish, try a first-class hamburger. You can cook these Nevada-style burgers on the stove, on an outdoor grill, or on a wood fire under the stars. (Have an adult help you with the cooking.)

Start with a pound of good-quality, lean ground beef. Ground top round steak is the best. You'll also want four sourdough buns or kaiser rolls. In a bowl, mix any combination of the following ingredients:

1 tsp. each mustard powder, chili powder, and/or cayenne pepper
2 tbsp. chopped fresh parsley
½ tbsp. Worcestershire sauce or barbecue sauce

With clean hands, gently knead the seasoning mixture into the ground beef. Handle it just enough to mix the ingredients loosely—too much handling can make the meat tough. Divide the seasoned beef into four lumps and pat each one into a flattened burger. Cook them until they are hot all the way through and done to your liking. Serve your burgers on toasted rolls. Nevada farmers grow plenty of potatoes and onions, so have a side order of french fries, or top your burger with a tangy onion slice.

Another key economic activity in Nevada is warehousing, or storing goods for businesses based all over the country. Low-cost land and labor make it easy to build large warehouses in the state, and the network of railways and interstate highways means that goods can be shipped from Nevada to almost anywhere in the West within a few days. Warehousing creates several thousand new jobs statewide each year.

The growth of Internet businesses, in which someone with a computer in a cabin in Alaska can offer goods for the whole world to buy, may mean even more demand for Nevada's warehousing and shipping services. Many retailers who do business in cyber-space are finding that Nevada is an economical place to carry out such real-world functions. In addition, business groups in Nevada are working to attract high-technology industries, such as computer-chip and software manufacturing. The tourism business has given Nevada its second golden boom. Some Nevadans want to make sure that the boom isn't followed by another big bust.

4 THE FASTEST-GROWING STATE

Nevada is a state that embraces contradictions, even thrives on them," exclaims Ron Dixon, a thirty-year resident of Reno. "We've got desert, but also Lake Tahoe, one of the most beautiful bodies of water in the world. We've got Las Vegas, the fastest-growing city in America, and we've also got ghost towns and some little towns that might turn into ghost towns. We've got recluses who live alone in shacks up in the mountains and come into town twice a year for supplies, and we've got celebrities and people from all over the world flocking to Vegas for big media events like boxing matches. But it's all Nevada."

BIG CITY, SMALL TOWN

Life in Nevada means many different things. Take Las Vegas. To a man from Mexico who works in a Vegas casino half of every year, the city represents opportunity—in six months he earns more than he would all year south of the border, and he can take the rest of the year off enjoying time with his family at home. "Maybe in a few years we will all come here to live and become Americans," says one Mexican worker. "Las Vegas is a good place for jobs."

Some people make the most of the city's economic boom while holding themselves apart from the Strip and all that it represents. "We operate totally outside the world of the casinos," says a father

Spanish musicians perform at Caesar's Palace in Las Vegas before a boxing match. Boxing and wrestling bouts attract large audiences to the city's auditoriums.

of three. "We just think of them as a blob of real estate downtown that we avoid with a passion." Seventeen-year-old Anya Margulies agrees. "It's like there are two cities here," she explains. "There's the Strip, the whole downtown. . . . It's really just for tourists. The real city, for people who live here, is hard to pin down. We hang out at different places and actually go out of town a lot."

Small towns, too, provoke a range of responses. "Wouldn't think of living anywhere else," says an old man who lives just outside tiny

Residents of Jarbidge pause on the main street to catch up on the local news. The pace of life is relaxed in such communities, and many Nevadans like it that way.

Austin, in the center of the state. "Life's just fine here. I know everyone, and everyone knows me." But small-town comfort can turn stifling. A thirteen-year-old girl from Tonopah, a town of about four thousand, complains, "This is the deadest place in the world. Imagine how bad it was before they had satellite dishes!"

PEOPLE AND WATER

Since 1980 Nevada's population has grown faster than that of any other state. And that growth is likely to continue. "There are a lot of reasons to move here," says a newcomer who relocated from New York to Reno. "There's no state income tax, housing prices are incredibly low, and the climate is great." Retirees, in particular, find Nevada's warm weather and low cost of living agreeable.

Most of the growth is concentrated in and around Las Vegas. "The city's spreading like a rash in almost all directions," laughs one longtime resident. A short drive out of Vegas reveals mile after

TEN LARGEST CITIES

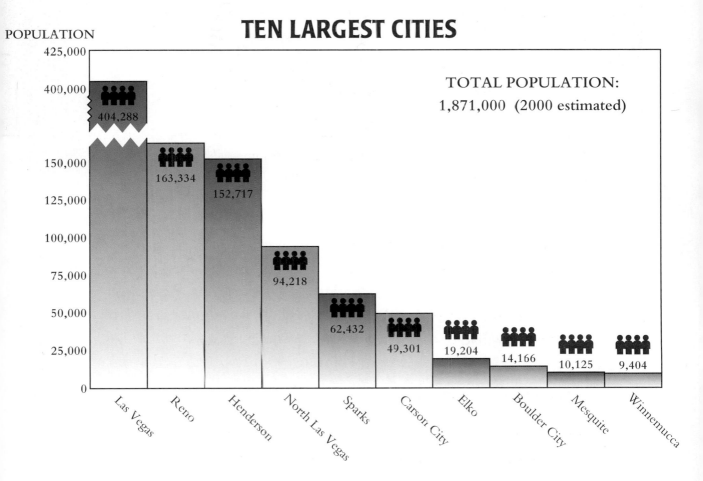

POPULATION

TOTAL POPULATION:
1,871,000 (2000 estimated)

Las Vegas 404,288
Reno 163,334
Henderson 152,717
North Las Vegas 94,218
Sparks 62,432
Carson City 49,301
Elko 19,204
Boulder City 14,166
Mesquite 10,125
Winnemucca 9,404

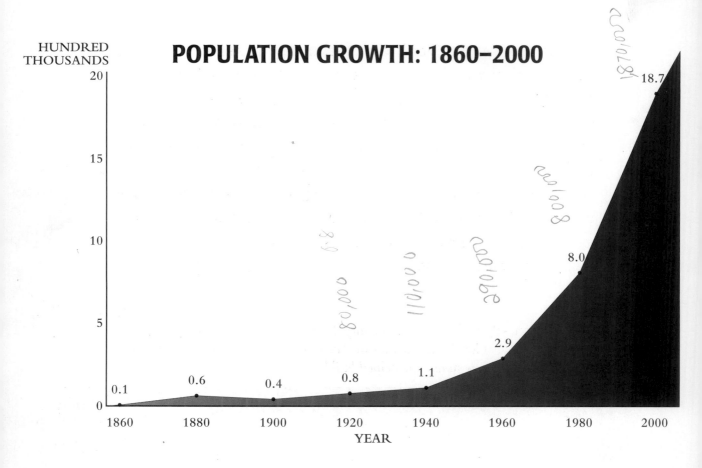

POPULATION GROWTH: 1860–2000

HUNDRED
THOUSANDS

20

15

10

5

0

0.1   0.6   0.4   0.8   1.1   2.9   8.0   18.7

1860   1880   1900   1920   1940   1960   1980   2000

YEAR

mile of new construction: town houses, apartment buildings, dozens of earth-toned, tile-roofed developments springing up almost overnight, each with carefully landscaped yards maintained by built-in sprinkler systems. Swimming pools twinkle under the desert sun. But where's the water coming from?

Las Vegas draws most of its water from Lake Mead, which was formed when Hoover Dam was built on the Colorado River. Under a federal agreement, Nevada shares the Colorado's water with seven other states. Officials estimate that by 2008 Nevada will be using its full share of the river's water. They have proposed drawing water from new sources, including the Virgin River and even the Columbia River in Washington, but such plans would involve costly construction projects, squabbles with other states over water rights, or both.

Officials have enacted some water-saving laws, such as banning the construction of new artificial lakes in the Las Vegas area. Hoping to avoid strict rules governing water use, the state encourages people to conserve water voluntarily. Many of the big water users—the golf

The rapid growth of Las Vegas is turning desert into suburbs. "I hope it goes on forever," says a local construction worker whose overtime pay allowed him to buy one of the new houses he helped build.

courses and the casinos with artificial lakes and waterfalls—already practice conservation, recycling and reusing their water. Home owners are less efficient. "The single biggest use of water when the temperature soars here is people watering their lawns," says one Las Vegas official. "And people overwater profusely. Some 64 percent of water is used by residents, and nearly half of that is wasted." To boost conservation efforts, water managers encourage xeriscaping, or "dry landscaping," designing yards with sand, rocks, and drought-resistant plants native to the region. But a drive through Las Vegas in 2000 revealed just a handful of xeriscaped yards amid hundreds of lush, green, well-watered lawns. Most had nothing and no one on them.

ETHNIC NEVADA

Nevada has a long history of ethnic diversity. During the 1860s the United States received a wave of immigrants from other shores, and many of them came to Nevada, working in the mines or on ranches and railroads. By 1870 Nevada had a larger proportion of immigrants in its population than any other state.

Irish, German, and Italian workers came to toil in the Comstock mines. Later mining booms drew many Greek and Eastern European immigrants. One distinctive group was the Basques, a people from the Pyrenees Mountains between France and Spain. They came to work the mines, but most had been sheepherders in their native land, and when the mines folded many of them stayed on as herdsmen and ranchers. They settled in and around Reno, Winnemucca, and Elko. All three cities still hold annual Basque

ETHNIC NEVADA

American Indian,
Inuit, Aleutian

Asian,
Pacific Islander

African
American

Hispanic

White

festivals, and Basque-inspired foods such as garlicky lamb and stews prepared with salted cod appear on their restaurant menus.

Although the European immigrants encountered some discrimination, they eventually found acceptance within the general population. Nonwhite newcomers were not always so fortunate. Chinese immigrants arrived during the Comstock era to build railroads and work in the mines. Racial hostility against them remained strong in Nevada, as in other parts of the West, and by 1900 many of them had left the state.

African Americans had arrived in Nevada even earlier, during the period of fur trapping and exploration. James Beckwourth, a black mountain man, pioneered a pass from the Truckee River through the Sierra Nevada. Jacob Dodson accompanied Frémont's expeditions. Black rancher Ben Palmer settled in the Carson Valley in

Basque children in Winnemucca, ready to dance in traditional costumes

1853; his family remained prominent in the valley for seventy years. Blacks entered Nevada during the mining booms, but in much smaller numbers than the European immigrants.

At the beginning of the twenty-first century, Nevada was still a predominantly white state. African Americans accounted for 7.6 percent of its population. The fastest-growing groups were Hispanic (14.5 percent) and Asian or Pacific Islander (4.6 percent). Many nonwhite Nevadans strive to find a balance between becoming part of mainstream Nevada society and maintaining their own cultural identity. Steven Kwon of Las Vegas's Asian Chamber of Commerce believes in the importance of ethnic ties, but also believes that Nevada's ethnic groups must see themselves as part of the larger whole. "We don't need a China Town or Korean Town. That's too isolated," he has said. "We Asian people are walking together with our community—the fastest-growing community."

Nevada's smallest ethnic group is made up of Native Americans, who total less than 2 percent of the state's population. When whites began settling Nevada, the Indians saw their way of life disrupted. Pushed to the margins of white society, the Indians have explored many different approaches to reclaiming their heritage and identity. Jack Wilson, a Nevada-born Northern Paiute raised by whites in the late nineteenth century, sought a spiritual solution, reviving a traditional ritual called the Ghost Dance, which Indians believed would link them to the powers of their ancestors and help them overpower the whites. Under the name Wovoka, he spread the Ghost Dance religion across the Great Plains in the 1880s. More recently, Nevada's Native Americans have turned to other ways of winning legal and economic power. They have launched lawsuits to regain greater control of traditional lands and waters. They have also formed intertribal organizations so that different groups can act together on political issues.

FESTIVALS AND FUN

For many Nevadans in pioneer days, culture consisted of a tattered newspaper or treasured book passed around a mining camp, and

A Native American woman at a tribal gathering. Native Americans are now Nevada's smallest minority, but their cultural influence is felt in all parts of the state.

most folks were too busy working to worry about recreation. Fortunately, times have changed.

Nevada's link with the performing arts stretches back to the

THE BURNING MAN

Nevada hosts many festivals that celebrate history, ethnic pride, or the arts. Perhaps the strangest is the Burning Man Festival, held in late summer or early fall in the Black Rock Desert in Nevada's northwestern corner.

The Burning Man tradition dates from 1986, when a San Franciscan named Larry Harvey built an eight-foot wooden figure and burned it on a local beach, to the delight of a handful of friends and passersby. By 1988 the figure, now called Burning Man, was thirty feet tall, and two hundred attended the ceremonial burning. Two years later California authorities banned the burning, and the ceremony moved to the inhospitable Black Rock Desert, where it has continued to grow. These days, the festival attracts more than 15,000 people.

"Burning Man is about building a community and building art," says Hilary Perkins, who has attended three festivals. "Everyone becomes an artist." People come from all over the world to construct artworks that are ritually burned on the final night of the event. They also perform plays, dances, and operas, and construct distinctive buildings and costumes, such as a hut made of old bathtubs or a suit made of glowing flexible plastic tubes called light-sticks. "They say extraterrestrials land in Nevada," Perkins laughs. "If so, they should come to Burning Man. They'd fit right in."

lavish performances in Virginia City's opera house in the 1860s. Today, cultural events include symphony, opera, and ballet productions in Las Vegas and Reno, a Shakespeare festival at Sand Harbor, one of the West's largest art shows in Boulder City, and not one but two cowboy poetry gatherings each year. Las Vegas is the

"Anybody who doesn't think rodeo is a major professional sport just hasn't been to a good one," said a nineteen-year-old fan in Reno a week after attending his thirteenth rodeo.

Music lovers gather for an outdoor concert on the shore of Lake Tahoe, at Sand Harbor State Park.

Hikers cross a snow patch on Wheeler Peak in Great Basin National Park, one of Nevada's most magnificent destinations for outdoor adventure.

hub of all kinds of entertainment, including annual festivals of jazz, Latin music festivals, and casino shows by world-famous musicians and magicians.

Las Vegas is also home to some highly publicized sports events, especially big-ticket boxing. Nevada has no major-league professional sports teams, but the state's devotion to college basketball is legendary, and teams from the University of Nevada's Las Vegas and

Reno campuses have loud, loyal followers. Plenty of other sports, some of them offbeat, take place in Nevada. A typical year's calendar might include golf tournaments, rodeos, shooting contests, balloon races, bike races. races on old-style, pump-operated railroad hand-cars, and even burro and camel races. And since it's Nevada, there's often heavy betting on the outcomes.

For those who want to be active, Nevada offers both highs and lows. The highs are the mountains. Western Nevada offers excellent skiing, especially around Lake Tahoe. "People don't always think of Nevada as the place for mountain adventures," says Jamie Weiss of San Francisco, who heads to Nevada each summer for a back-packing trip. "As a result, you can find some of the West's most uncrowded, unspoiled country here." The lows are the river canyons and deserts, which offer hiking, biking, and camping opportunities but require careful preparation to avoid the possibly deadly dangers of heat and thirst. As the early trappers, pioneers, and miners discovered, Nevada's landscape can be harsh—but to those who enter it with respect, that landscape offers magnificent scenery, solitude, and glimpses of a natural world that existed long before the busy streets and bright lights of the cities.

5 NOTABLE NEVADANS

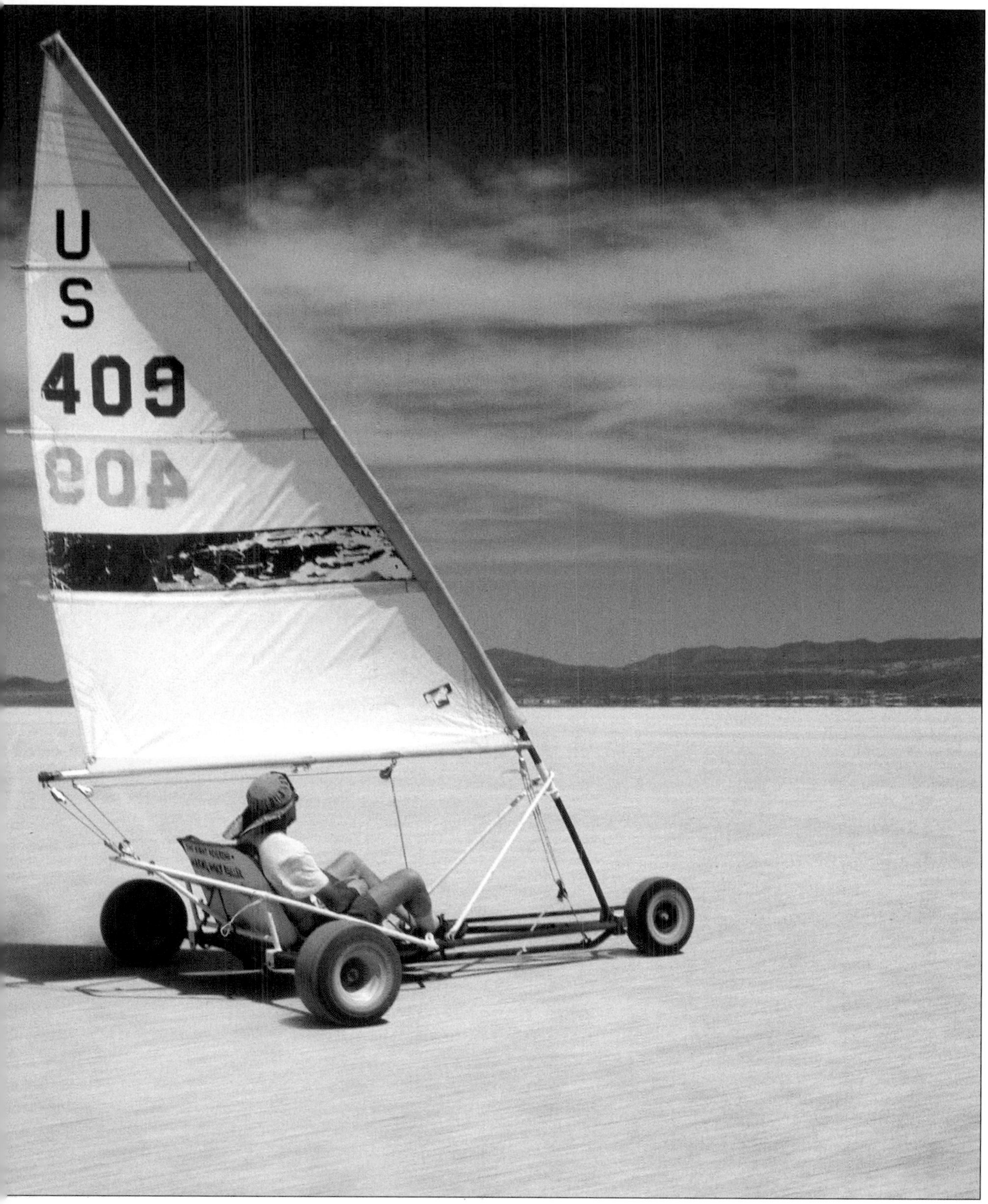
US
409

Some remarkable talents have sprouted and flourished in Nevada's arid soil. The achievements of these Nevadans have reached beyond the borders of their state to touch people's hearts and change the world.

ARTISTS AND WRITERS

One of Nevada's greatest artists was a Washo woman named Dat-So-La-Lee, who lived from around 1835 until 1925. Dat-So-La-Lee spent most of her life in the woods of western Nevada. Like many Washo women, she was a highly skilled basket weaver. Beyond that, however, she possessed a spark of creative genius that made her baskets superb works of art.

Dat-So-La-Lee's work was so detailed that she sometimes fit a hundred tiny stitches into an inch. It took as much as a year to complete one basket. Some creations were given a name, such as "Migration" or "Stars Shine over the Graves of My Ancestors."

During her lifetime, Dat-So-La-Lee became so well known that one of her baskets fetched the astounding price of $1,500. When she died, her last unfinished basket, "Friendship," was buried with her. Since that time, the balance, beauty, and grace of her work have continued to captivate admirers. Today Dat-So-La-Lee's

Washo basket maker Dat-So-La-Lee, photographed around 1900, was one of the foremost practitioners of an elegant and useful art.

baskets are owned by a number of museums, including the Smithsonian Institution in Washington, D.C.

Nevada's distinctive flavor emerges from the pages of books by writers from the state. One of Nevada's best-known literary figures was Walter van Tilburg Clark, author of novels and short stories with western settings and moral themes. Although he was born in Maine in 1909, Clark grew up in Reno. His 1945 novel *The City of Trembling Leaves*, which tells the story of a boy's coming of age, is set there. Clark is most famous for *The Ox-Bow*

Walter van Tilburg Clark spent years in other states but considered Nevada his home. Many of his writings capture the flavor of its immense skies and austere landscapes.

Incident, the tale of a frontier lynching, and *The Track of the Cat*, which describes a hunt for a mountain lion during a blizzard.

SPORTS HEROES

In the late twentieth century, two sports giants emerged from Nevada.

Cyclist Greg LeMond moved to Reno with his family in 1969, when he was eight years old. Even as a kid, he loved riding his bicycle and could pedal hard for many miles. LeMond began making his mark as a serious cyclist in 1977, when he won the junior national championships. Two years later he won the junior

SWEET PROMISED LAND

Robert Laxalt wrote several books about Nevada. One of them, *Sweet Promised Land*, tells of growing up with his Basque father. In this much-loved volume, Laxalt celebrates his Basque heritage but recognizes Nevada as his family's true home.

Robert seldom saw his father while growing up, because the elder Laxalt was usually out with his herds:

> My father was a sheep herder, and his home was the hills. So it began when he was a boy in the misted Pyrenees of France, and so it was to be for the most of his lifetime in the lonely Sierra Nevada. And seeing him in a moment's pause on a high ridge, with the wind tearing at his wild thickness of iron-gray hair and flattening his clothes to his lean frame, you could understand why this was what he was meant to be.

Describing how Nevada had become his father's true home, Laxalt writes;

> I saw the West rising up at dawn with an awesome vastness of deserts and mighty mountain ranges. I saw a band of sheep winding their way down a lonely mountain ravine of sagebrush and pine, and I smelled their dust and heard the muted bleating and the lovely tinkle of their bells. I saw a man in crude garb with a walking stick following after with his dog, and once he stopped to mark the way of the land. Then I saw a cragged face that that land had filled with hope and torn with pain, had changed from young to old, and in the end had claimed.

world championships. He soon moved to Europe, where the sport of bicycle racing is highly regarded.

Europeans called LeMond "the American" and questioned whether he could compete with their highly trained riders. In 1984 he showed them that he could by coming in third in the 2,500-mile, three-week Tour de France, the world's most famous bicycle race. Two years later, LeMond became the first American to win the Tour de France. Overnight, he was recognized as one of the world's top athletes. Then tragedy struck. While hunting, LeMond was accidentally shot in the back. Doctors saved his life but

Greg LeMond wears the winner's yellow jersey at the conclusion of the Tour de France. Despite a serious injury and illness, he won this grueling bicycle race three times.

could not remove all of the shotgun pellets. LeMond eventually recovered, but most believed his cycling career was over.

They were wrong. With fierce dedication and a strict training schedule, LeMond prepared to return to competitive cycling, and in 1989 he again entered the Tour de France. With a burst of extraordinary energy on the last day, he seized the lead and won by eight seconds. LeMond won the Tour de France for a third time in 1990.

Despite hard training, LeMond's famed endurance began to decline. In 1992 he had to quit in the middle of the Tour de France. Never again could he muster his former strength and speed. Finally, doctors discovered that LeMond had developed a rare disease that makes it hard for him to turn food into energy. No longer able to perform at his best, the first American cycling hero retired from the sport in 1994. Knowing that his illness might get worse, he has vowed to treasure every day. "The years go by awfully fast," says LeMond. "That has changed the way I look at things. I want to spend the next ten or fifteen years enjoying myself and doing things I might not get to do when I'm old."

Like LeMond, Andre Agassi became world famous for his unique approach to his sport. Agassi was born in Las Vegas in 1970. His father loved tennis and taught his four children the sport. He drilled them on a tennis court in their backyard, using machines that spat out tennis balls faster than the kids could hit them. Andre showed the most promise, and at age thirteen he was sent to Florida to attend a tennis school. Life at the tennis academy wasn't always smooth. Agassi felt the pressure of his father's expectations and of his own competitive nature. As his game continued to develop, so did the colorful, rebellious style that would become his trademark.

Andre Agassi was trained from childhood to be a tennis star. His colorful personality seems to reflect the showiness and liveliness of Las Vegas, his hometown.

When he was sixteen, Agassi turned pro. By the late 1980s he had become a superstar, almost as famous for his good looks as for his hard-hitting game. "Seeing Agassi play in person is a little bit like attending a Beatles concert during the 1960s," declared a writer for the *Los Angeles Times*. Hordes of girls screamed and threw flowers when he appeared on the court.

Agassi's career has been a roller-coaster ride. One high point came in the early 1990s, when Agassi won three of the four tournaments that together make up tennis's Grand Slam. He won Wimbledon in 1992, the U.S. Open in 1994, and the Australian Open in 1995. Then came a decline, and Agassi almost seemed to be dropping out of the sport. By the end of 1997 he was ranked 110 among the world's professional players—a very low ranking for a former champion.

But two years later, Agassi made a stunning comeback. He had gathered his ambition, sharpened his focus, and trained for up to five hours a day, including running sprints up what he calls Magic Mountain, a hill in Las Vegas, the city where he still makes his home. In 1999 Agassi won the French Open and the U.S. Open. Whatever Agassi's future may hold, he has already proven himself one of the tennis greats.

FIGHTING FOR A CAUSE

Some people might have considered Velma Johnston an unlikely hero—before she showed how dedicated and hardworking she could be when fighting to end the slaughter of wild horses.

Born in Reno in 1912 to a ranching family, Johnston became ill when she was eleven. The crippling disease polio forced her to spend half a year in a body cast and left her disabled, frequently suffering from pain and exhaustion. Her spirit, however, was strong.

Johnston's crusade began in 1950. While driving to work one day, she noticed a trail of blood coming from a livestock truck that was carrying horses. Disturbed, she followed the truck to a slaughter-house and was horrified by what she saw: frightened horses trampling younger ones, a stallion with its eyes shot out, animals whose feet were worn to bloody stumps because they had been forced to run almost to death. She discovered that armed hunters were using planes and jeeps to round up wild horses. Most of them ended up in pet food.

"I went home that night and I knew I couldn't live with myself unless I did something about it," Johnston later said. "I decided right there and then that I would not rest until I had done everything humanly possible to stop such atrocities." Johnston learned that the law allowed mustangs to be hunted like pests. Many ranchers were glad to be rid of them, although the mustangs interfered very little with cattle and sheep ranching. The Bureau of Land Management (BLM), which oversees the use of public land, encouraged the extermination of the mustangs. One BLM official mocked Johnston's

Velma Johnston, shown with one of the mustangs she rescued from slaughter, proudly accepted the scornful nickname Wild Horse Annie as she carried her crusade all the way to Congress.

crusade by calling her Wild Horse Annie. His mockery backfired, however, because she adopted the nickname with pride and used it to rally support for her cause.

Johnston fought tirelessly to draw attention to the plight of the mustangs. She made speeches all across the West and testified before a congressional committee, handing the startled congressmen photographs of the bodies of dead and mutilated horses. All this activity made Johnston unpopular in some quarters. In a letter to a Nevada paper, one disgruntled citizen warned, "Wild Horse Annie will be called Dead Horse Annie in a very few short years."

But in 1959, thanks to Johnston's efforts, Congress passed a bill later called the Wild Horse Annie Act. It outlawed the hunting of mustangs from planes or motorized vehicles on public land. The law did not, however, prevent the hunting of wild horses by other means or on private land. Marguerite Henry, the author of several popular children's books about horses, wrote *Mustang: Wild Spirit of the West*, the story of Wild Horse Annie's girlhood and her fight to save the mustangs. The book won thousands of young supporters to the cause. Many of them wrote letters to Annie—and to their legislators.

In 1971, Wild Horse Annie again testified in Washington. This time Congress passed a law banning the capture, harassment, or killing of wild mustangs and burros on public land. Before her death in 1977, Johnston created an organization called the Wild Horse Organized Assistance (WHOA), to watch for violations of laws protecting these wild animals—laws that she had brought into being because she could not rest after what she saw on her way to work one day.

6 SILVER STATE ROAD TRIP

"**N**evada will surprise you" says Carla Druckerman of Pennsylvania, after touring the Silver State. "But if you want to see more than one side of the place, you've got to cover some ground." The state's tourism commission divides Nevada into six territories, each with attractions all its own.

INDIAN TERRITORY

Unlike the other five territories, Indian Territory has no specific location—it covers the entire state and includes not just the Native American reservations but also other places representing Indian life and culture, past and present.

Rock walls throughout Nevada are marked with petroglyphs, images chipped into the rock by Indians in the distant past. The symbols of people, animals, hands, and the sun seem hauntingly familiar. Other images are more mysterious: spirals, wavy lines, horned humans. They tease us with their mystery, for no one, not even modern Indians, knows for certain what they mean or why long-ago people labored for many hours to create them. Some of the most spectacular petroglyphs are preserved in Valley of Fire State Park near the town of Overton, northeast of Las Vegas. The park is a canyon of red sandstone that glows like flames in the sunlight. Also in Overton is the Lost City Museum of Archaeology,

Rock walls in Valley of Fire State Park bear mysterious petroglyphs, images left behind by the region's Native American inhabitants.

which explains the history and culture of the Anasazi. The Stewart Indian Museum in Carson City focuses on more recent Indian tribes. It houses a collection of arrowheads and other stone tools, with explanations of how they were made and used.

If you visit Pyramid Lake, you will enter Indian Territory—literally.

The lake is on a Paiute reservation. The northern part of the lake is closed to visitors, but you can view its southern shores from a scenic roadway or, with a permit, fish for its forty-pound trout.

Nevada's Native Americans hold dozens of gatherings each year. Some are traditional religious celebrations, while others emphasize handicrafts, sports, or feasts. Many of these events, such as the Mother Earth Awakening Pow Wow held each spring in Carson City, are open to visitors. Most feature traditional music and dancing. The dancers wear dramatic fringed, beaded, and feathered costumes and headdresses. Some outfits, made of traditional materials, are shaded

Dancers at a powwow, an Indian gathering that may also feature sports, feasts, and sacred ceremonies.

red and brown like the earth itself. Other outfits feature new materials, allowing the dancers to create swirling, exciting patterns in vivid colors such as hot pink and electric blue.

LAS VEGAS TERRITORY

Las Vegas Territory is the small but lively southern triangle of Nevada. "What can you say about Las Vegas?" sighed one travel writer. "It's impossible to sum up." Many books have been written about the city's attractions, which are constantly changing. By the early twenty-first century, massive theme resorts had begun to replace some of the older, more traditional neon-and-cocktail-lounge casinos. One such resort, the Luxor, has an Egyptian theme and is housed in a black glass structure that is the fourth-largest pyramid in the world. Paris Las Vegas is a huge hotel casino with its own Eiffel Tower (smaller than the original in Paris, France). The Venetian echoes the Italian city of Venice, right down to a canal that winds among its shops and restaurants. The scale of Las Vegas, though, is entirely American—the Venetian has more hotel rooms in a single building than there are in the whole city of Venice.

These buildings contain hotel and meeting rooms, restaurants, and stores as well as the casinos themselves. The casinos, though, are a world apart, especially the older ones. Generally smoky, they have no windows and seem to lack all connection with the outside world. "In here, under these lights, it's always eleven o'clock at night," a grandmotherly woman chuckles as she works a row of the Golden Nugget's slot machines before breakfast. The constant electronic beeping and mechanical bonging of hundreds

Stretching enormous concrete paws toward the Strip, a replica of Egypt's Sphinx guards the portals of the Luxor casino.

of slot machines drowns out the piped-in music. Some casinos, laid out in many branching chambers, feel like mazes. It's not always easy to find your way out.

These days, the casinos are only part of what Las Vegas offers. As you stroll along the Strip you can see circus acts, simulated volcanic explosions, or actors in pirate battles. You can bungee jump, ride a roller coaster around an imitation New York, or take a virtual-reality trip into space. You can stuff yourself satisfyingly and inexpensively at "all-you-can-eat" buffet restaurants—every casino has one.

Or you can get out of town and see some of southern Nevada's other sights. Hoover Dam remains as impressive now as when it was the world's biggest construction project. The Hard Hat Tour takes you deep inside the dam for a close-up look at its workings. Nearby, scenic roads wind along the shoreline of Lake Mead, a refreshing blue

When it was being built in the 1930s, Hoover Dam was the world's largest construction project. Today it is still an impressive sight.

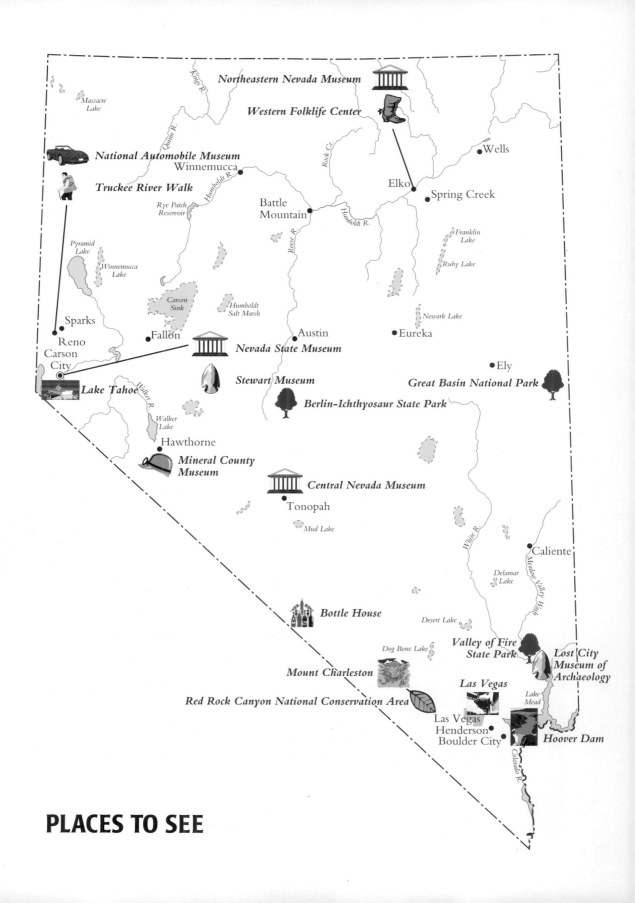

Northeastern Nevada Museum

Western Folklife Center

National Automobile Museum

Truckee River Walk

Wells

Winnemucca

Elko

Spring Creek

Massacre Lake

Quinn R.

Rock Cr.

Humboldt R.

Rye Patch Reservoir

Battle Mountain

Humboldt R.

Franklin Lake

Pyramid Lake

Winnemucca Lake

Reese R.

Ruby Lake

Carson Sink

Humboldt Salt Marsh

Newark Lake

Sparks

Fallon

Austin

Eureka

Reno

Carson City

Nevada State Museum

Ely

Great Basin National Park

Lake Tahoe

Stewart Museum

Walker R.

Walker Lake

Berlin-Ichthyosaur State Park

Hawthorne

Mineral County Museum

Central Nevada Museum

Tonopah

Mud Lake

White R.

Caliente

Delamar Lake

Meadow Valley Wash

Bottle House

Desert Lake

Dog Bone Lake

Valley of Fire State Park

Lost City Museum of Archaeology

Mount Charleston

Las Vegas

Lake Mead

Red Rock Canyon National Conservation Area

Las Vegas

Henderson

Boulder City

Hoover Dam

Colorado R.

PLACES TO SEE

gem in a parched landscape. In the other direction, on Las Vegas's northwestern horizon, a tree-covered peak beckons. It is Mount Charleston, a cool oasis for picnicking, hiking, or camping. Just west of the city is the Red Rock Canyon National Conservation Area, a stretch of dramatic terrain that delights rock climbers, cyclists, and hikers. "I don't think I could stand to live in Las Vegas if this place weren't here," says Lauren Ganz, who rides her bike through the canyon three evenings a week. "It's the perfect medicine when I've had too much city and too many people."

PIONEER TERRITORY

Pioneer Territory covers a broad swath of south-central Nevada, from Walker Lake in the west to the Utah border in the east. Tonopah and Goldfield, the sites of big mining booms around 1900, are located in Pioneer Territory. So are a fair number of Nevada's seven hundred or so ghost towns. While a few of these old settlements are run as tourist attractions, complete with restored buildings, restaurants, and motels, most have been left in a state of slow, gentle decay.

Many ghost towns consist of nothing more than a few crumbling walls, a dried-out well, and perhaps the traces of a long-vanished road. Some of the most remote ghost towns, seldom visited, don't even have names anymore. Others are better known because of their unusual features. In 1908 Rhyolite was the second-largest city in Nevada, with hundreds of houses, saloons, and even an opera house. But the mines failed, and by 1914 only three hundred people remained. Today just a few structures survive, including

ON THE EXTRATERRESTRIAL HIGHWAY

For years rumors have flown about mysterious flying objects and lights in the night sky along state highway 375, which runs through central Nevada along the northern edge of Nellis Air Force Range. Some people claim that the region is visited by aliens in UFOs, others that the "UFOs" are really top-secret experimental military aircraft. Still others point to the lack of real evidence for any unusual happenings and say that the whole thing is bunk.

Still, the rumors have attracted conspiracy buffs and curiosity seekers of all sorts for years. So many people were driving up and down 375 in the hope of spotting a UFO that Nevada officials decided to take advantage of the publicity. They designated the road the Extraterrestrial Highway and prepared brochures promoting it to tourists. The owners of an inn in Rachel, the only town along the highway, jumped into the act by renaming their place the Little A-Le-Inn (for "alien") and proclaiming "Extraterrestrials welcome!" The restaurant's gift shop sells a wide array of UFO-related merchandise, from T-shirts to keychains to maps of the "best viewing spots" along the road. Are the people who visit the inn believers hoping to see a spaceship or skeptics who just want a good laugh? The inn's owners say it's about fifty-fifty.

The Bottle House in Rhyolite, one of the most famous abandoned buildings in the West, is made almost entirely out of empty bottles.

the old railroad depot and the Bottle House, which miners built out of empty bottles. At the northern edge of Pioneer Territory is Berlin-Icthyosaur State Park, which includes the remains of the old silver-mining town of Berlin and a fossil dig where scientists have found the remains of ancient ichthyosaurs.

You can learn about the ghost towns and the heritage of central Nevada at two museums. The Mineral County Museum in Hawthorne displays mining and railroad equipment from Nevada's early days, along with clothing, furniture, and other everyday possessions used by pioneers. The Central Nevada Museum in Tonopah focuses on mining and the boomtowns. Ore-crushers and other huge pieces of old mining equipment dot the museum's grounds.

PONY EXPRESS TERRITORY

North of Pioneer Territory is Pony Express Territory, a strip of basin-and-range terrain that extends across the center of Nevada. U.S. Highway 50 runs through this part of Nevada along the route once taken by riders for the Pony Express and Overland Stage companies, the mail carriers of the Old West. Years ago *Life* magazine called Highway 50, which runs for several hundred miles through this wide-open, uncrowded region, "the Loneliest Road in America." The name stuck, and today at gas stations and cafes along the way you can buy souvenir shirts or bumper stickers that boast "I Survived the Loneliest Road."

The only national park entirely within the state of Nevada is located in Pony Express Territory. It is Great Basin National Park, one of the least crowded national parks in the country. "It's kind of out of the way, pretty far from any big city," explains Kathleen Worley, who grew up in Nevada. "You have to make an effort to get there, but it's well worth it." Great Basin surrounds Wheeler Peak, a massive mountain that rises majestically above the surrounding landscape. The glacier near the mountain's summit is the southernmost such ice formation in the United States. The park also includes the Lehman Caves, a magnificent underground treasure with some extremely rare rock formations. The flat, plate-like shapes called shields occur in only a handful of other caves worldwide.

If you're driving on the Loneliest Road, you're bound to stop in Eureka, a tiny town that was once a lead-mining center. Eureka's centerpiece is its 1880 opera house, which has a magnificent painted curtain dating from 1924.

A rider reenacts the journey of the Pony Express mail carriers, who galloped across central Nevada in 1860 and 1861.

COWBOY COUNTRY

The northern third of Nevada is Cowboy Country. As its name suggests, this part of Nevada is where the state's ranching is concentrated. Horseback riding, roping, and other cowboy skills are still part of everyday life for many women and men. The city of Elko, once a stopover for wagon trains, is now the center of a movement to preserve and celebrate the area's heritage through events

The Ruby Mountains loom above the flatlands in the northeastern part of the state, offering a haven for wildlife and wilderness lovers.

such as the Cowboy Poetry Gathering, the Basque Festival, and the Silver State Stampede Rodeo. Its Northeastern Nevada Museum has exhibits about local Native American, pioneer, mining, and ranching history as well as the area's wildlife. The Western Folklife Center is dedicated to preserving ranching culture, including handicrafts such as whittling.

Cowboy Country also includes outdoor attractions. The Ruby

Mountains, south of Elko, are the wettest and greenest range in Nevada. They attract hikers in the summertime, and in winter skiers airlift in by helicopter to carve the powdery snow. Near the Rubies is glacier-carved Lamoille Canyon, where you can drive through a vista of dramatic stone peaks and cliffs.

RENO-TAHOE TERRITORY

Reno-Tahoe Territory runs up the western border of Nevada from Lake Tahoe to the Oregon border. The lake is one of Nevada's most beautiful sights, a deep gem of cool sapphire water backed by the forested slopes of the Sierra Nevada. Lake Tahoe has long been famed for its invigorating climate and bracing air. Author Mark Twain declared in the nineteenth century, "Three months of camp life on Lake Tahoe would restore an Egyptian mummy to his pristine vigor, and give him an appetite like an alligator." Summer boating, winter skiing on the surrounding mountains, and casinos along the shore make Lake Tahoe an all-purpose recreation center.

Nine miles from the lake is Carson City, the state capital. Its premier attraction is the Nevada State Museum. Among the museum's holdings are baskets made by Washo artist Dat-So-La-Lee. The nearby Nevada State Railroad Museum displays more than sixty pieces of train equipment from the Virginia and Truckee Railroad and other Nevada lines, which hauled ore from the Comstock mines. Some pieces still function, and you can take a short ride along a stretch of the old track.

Reno, which proudly calls itself the Biggest Little City in the World, is a major gambling center. Reno has other attractions, how-

Volunteers operate a turntable to shift an 1888 steam locomotive at the Nevada State Railroad Museum, which preserves the memory of the time when trains transformed the West.

ever. The Nevada Historical Society Museum, founded in 1904, is Nevada's oldest museum and contains a library of documents dating from 1859. More than two hundred antique or rare cars are garaged in the National Automobile Museum, devoted to America's love affair with the automobile. One of Reno's most distinctive features is the Truckee River Walk, a decorative marble path along the Truckee River, which winds through the city.

North of Reno is Pyramid Lake, and still farther north is one of the emptiest corners of the state, a region of playas and dry mountain ranges, of unpaved roads and long, long stretches between towns. This austere region captures an essential part of Nevada's character. Fast-growing southern Nevada is "where the people and the power are," wrote author David Thomson, after exploring Nevada's high-

Reno's slogan captures its desire to be both a friendly small town and a glittering entertainment center. Within its borders, Nevada has plenty of room for both.

ways and byways. "Yet all the rest of the state . . . to the last bit of the northwest corner, where there is not even one small place to name, is Nevada too. And the emptiness is vital, even if it exists only as a warning or a signal to the bustling, expanding south."

THE FLAG: *The Nevada flag was designed in 1929 and modified in 1991. It has a cobalt blue background with a silver star between two branches of sagebrush in its upper-left corner. Above the star is a scroll bearing the words* Battle Born. *Below it is the name* Nevada

THE SEAL: *The state seal contains a group of pictures symbolizing Nevada. In the foreground is a plow with sheaves of wheat, representing agriculture. In the center of the seal, a mine shaft, a train crossing a trestle, and a building with a smokestack represent Nevada industry. Behind them, the sun peaks out behind snow-capped mountains. Underneath these images is a scroll with the state motto, "All for Our Country."*

STATE SURVEY

Statehood: October 31, 1864

Origin of Name: *Nevada* is a Spanish word meaning "snowcapped"

Nicknames: Sagebrush State, Silver State, Battle-Born State

Capital: Carson City

Motto: All for Our Country

Bird: Mountain bluebird

Animal: Desert bighorn sheep

Flower: Sagebrush

Trees: Single-leaf piñon, bristlecone pine

Fish: Lahontan cutthroat trout

Fossil: Ichthyosaur

Precious Stone: Virgin Valley black fire opal

Reptile: Desert tortoise

Bluebird

Sagebrush

"HOME, MEANS NEVADA"

The Nevada legislature adopted "Home, Means Nevada" as the official state song on February 6, 1933.

Home, means Ne - va - da, Home, means the hills, Home, means the sage and the

pines, Out by the Truck - ee's sil - ver - y rills,

Out where the sun al - ways shines. There is the land that

I love the best, Fair - er than all I can see.

Right in the heart of the gold - en west: Home, means Ne - va - da to me.

Rock: Sandstone

Metal: Silver

GEOGRAPHY

Highest Point: 13,143 feet above sea level, at Boundary Peak

Lowest Point: 470 feet about sea level, on the Colorado River in Clark County

Area: 110,540 square miles

Greatest Distance, North to South: 478 miles

Greatest Distance, East to West: 318 miles

Bordering States: Oregon and Idaho to the north, California to the west and south, Arizona and Utah to the east

Hottest Recorded Temperature: 125°F at Laughlin on June 29, 1994

Coldest Recorded Temperature: -50°F at San Jacinto on January 8, 1937

Average Annual Precipitation: 7 inches

Major Rivers: Bruneau, Carson, Colorado, Humboldt, Jarbidge, Muddy, Owyhee, Truckee, Virgin, Walker

Major Lakes: Franklin, Lamoille, Liberty, Mead, Mohave, Pyramid, Ruby, Rye Patch Reservoir, Tahoe, Topaz, Walker

Trees: alder, aspen, bristlecone pine, chokecherry, cottonwood, fir, hemlock, juniper, spruce, willow

Wild Plants: cactus, creosote, greasewood, Joshua tree, mesquite, sagebrush, saltbush, yucca

Cactus

Animals: badger, beaver, bighorn sheep, coyote, elk, garter snake, Gila monster, mink, mule deer, desert tortoise, muskrat, mustang, porcupine, pronghorn antelope, raccoon, rattlesnake, red fox, skunk, tortoise, wild burro

Birds: eagle, falcon, grouse, mountain bluebird, owl, partridge, pelican, pheasant, quail, sage hen

Fish: bass, carp, catfish, crappie, trout

Endangered Animals: Ash Meadows Amargosa pupfish, Ash Meadows speckled dace, bonytail chub, Clover Valley speckled dace, cui-ui, Devils Hole pupfish, Hiko White River springfish, Independence Valley speckled dace, Moapa dace, Pahranagat roundtail chub, Pahrump poolfish, razorback sucker, Virgin River chub, Warm Springs pupfish, White River spinedace, White River springfish, woundfin

Warm Springs pupfish

Endangered Plants: Amargosa niterwort, steamboat buckwheat

TIMELINE

Nevada History

ca. 300 B.C.–A.D. 1150 Anasazi live in southwestern Nevada

1600s Paiute, Shoshone, and Washo Indians live in what will become Nevada

1776 Francisco Garcés, a Spanish priest, possibly becomes the first European to pass through Nevada territory

1826 Mountain man Jedediah Smith crosses southern Nevada

1843 John C. Frémont maps the Great Basin

1848 Nevada becomes U.S. territory under the Treaty of Guadalupe-Hidalgo

1859 Miners discover the Comstock Lode, bringing a rush of gold and silver prospectors to western Nevada

1860 Comstock miners fight the Paiutes in the Pyramid Lake War

1864 Nevada becomes the 36th state

1868 The transcontinental railroad crosses Nevada

1874 Pyramid Lake and Walker Indian Reservations are created

1880–1894 The Comstock Lode and other mines peter out; around 15,000 people leave Nevada

1900 Silver is found at Tonopah and gold at Goldfield; mining revives

1907 Newlands irrigation project begins, transporting water from the Truckee River to the Fallon area for farming

1909 Nevada passes a law against gambling

1931 Nevada makes gambling legal again

1936 Boulder Dam, now known as Hoover Dam, is completed

1951 The U.S. Atomic Energy Commission starts testing nuclear weapons in southern Nevada

1963 The U.S. Supreme Court settles a dispute between Arizona, California and Nevada over the use of the Colorado River

1967 Nevada passes a law allowing corporations to own casinos

1971 The Robert B. Griffith Water Project is completed, helping supply the Las Vegas area with water from Lake Mead

1980 Nevada passes conservation laws to keep Lake Tahoe clean

1983 Barbara Vucanovich becomes the first woman to represent Nevada in Congress

1986 Great Basin National Park is created

ECONOMY

Agricultural Products: alfalfa, barley, cattle, chickens, corn, hay, hogs, horses, oats, potatoes, rye, sheep, wheat

Manufactured Products: concrete, food products, machinery, printed material

Sheep

Natural Resources: barite, coal, copper, diatomite, gold, gypsum, iron, limestone, magnesium, manganese, mercury, molybdenum, oil, sand and gravel, silver, tungsten, uranium, zinc

Business and Trade: advertising, communication, entertainment, finance, gambling, insurance, real estate, tourism, transportation, warehousing, wholesale and retail trade

CALENDAR OF CELEBRATIONS

Cowboy Poetry Gathering Cowpokes from around the country gather in Elko in January for a weeklong poetry jamboree. This celebration of Western culture features poetry readings, workshops, concerts, and art exhibits dedicated to the spirit of the open range.

Chariot Races Each January an ancient Roman sport is revived as horse-drawn chariots clatter around a race track in Wells. The night before people place bets on their favorite teams.

Cinco de Mayo Every year around May 5, a Mexican national holiday, Las Vegas remembers its Hispanic heritage with a weekend of Mexican food, music, and dancing.

National Basque Festival Elko's Basque community celebrates its history and culture with a weekend of traditional food, music, dancing, and sporting competitions in June.

Jim Butler Days Tonopah hosts the state mining championships during this July festival, named after the prospector who discovered silver there in 1900.

Lake Tahoe Shakespeare Festival at Sand Harbor In July and August, award-winning actors perform plays by William Shakespeare at Sand Harbor Beach State Park on the north shore of Lake Tahoe.

Spirit of Wovoka Days Powwow Yerington pays tribute to the Paiute mystic who launched the Ghost Dance movement during this August festival highlighting Native American arts, crafts, and dancing.

International Camel Races In 1959 a Virginia City paper printed a phony announcement about this wacky event—and later decided it was a good idea. Since then, camel jockeys from around the globe have been charging across the Nevada desert each September.

Genoa Candy Dance More than 4,000 pounds of candy is sold each September at this popular small-town festival. Visitors can also shop for arts and crafts and socialize at the Saturday-night buffet dinner.

Professional Bull Riders Tour October brings 45 of the world's best bull riders to Las Vegas, where they compete for the international title and a $1 million prize.

Professional Bull Riders Tour

Nevada Day Celebration and Parade The last weekend in October, Carson City celebrates the day Nevada became a state with a huge parade, the 1864 Ball, where guests dance wearing the fashions of the times, and other festivities.

Fisherman's Holiday Derby Champion anglers compete to see who can catch the biggest cutthroat trout during this November event on Walker Lake near Hawthorne.

National Finals Rodeo Las Vegas hosts the world's biggest rodeo each December with ten days of roping and riding, performances by the nation's top country and western musicians, and a Christmas gift show where visitors can shop for western wear.

STATE STARS

Andre Agassi (1970–   ), who was born in Las Vegas, grew up to become one of the best tennis players of the 1990s. Agassi is one of only five pros in the history of the game to win all four grand slam titles, taking the crown at Wimbledon, the U.S. Open, the Australian Open, and the French Open. Known for his bold playing style, he surprised the world by making a spectacular comeback after a three-year slump in the middle of the decade.

Phyllis Barber (1943–   ) is the author of many books about life in Nevada. Her 1992 book *How I Got Cultured: A Nevada Memoir* describes her childhood in Boulder City and Las Vegas.

Lucius Beebe (1902–1966) was a prolific writer and journalist who was known for his dashing style. In 1950 he moved from New York to Virgina City, where he bought the *Territorial Enterprise*, a newspaper that had fallen out of print. Under his direction, it soon became the most popular weekly in the West. Beebe was also a railroad buff, and he wrote many books on the subject, as well as articles for such widely read magazines as *Newsweek* and *Saturday Review*.

Walter van Tilburg Clark (1909–1971) was the author of many novels and short stories set in the American West. His best known work, *The Ox-Bow Incident*, tells the story of a frontier lynching. *The City of Trembling Leaves*, published in 1945, takes place in Reno, where he lived for many years.

Dat-So-La-Lee (c. 1835–1925) was a Washo basket maker from western Nevada whose beautiful designs won national acclaim. Her baskets were so detailed and distinctive that her fame spread far beyond the Washo tribe, and many are on display in museums today.

Dan De Quille (1829–1898) was nineteenth-century Nevada's most popular writer. An East Coast native, he was drawn to Nevada by stories of the Comstock Lode. De Quille edited Virginia City's *Territorial*

Enterprise off and on for more than thirty years, presenting vivid accounts of life around the mines. During that time, he trained a young reporter named Samuel Clemens, who went on to international stardom as the author Mark Twain.

Dan De Quille

Howard Hughes

Howard Hughes (1905–1976) was an industrialist, an aviator, an aircraft designer, and one of the twentieth century's most eccentric billionaires. Hughes began buying Las Vegas casinos in 1966 and helped clean up the city's image as a place to visit and be entertained. He lived for several years in seclusion at Las Vegas's Desert Inn.

Will James (1892–1942) was a writer and a cowboy. He was also a drifter, and was arrested for cattle rustling in 1914 and spent 15 months in the Nevada State Prison. After his release he lived on odd jobs until his first book, *Cowboys North and South*, earned him enough money to buy land in the Washoe Valley. James is best known for his 1926 book *Smoky, the Cowhorse*, which won a Newbery Medal for children's literature.

Velma Johnston (1912–1977) dedicated her life to the protection of the wild horses and burros that roam the American West. Johnston grew up on a ranch in Reno, where she developed a love for horses. When she learned that mustangs were being hunted down and slaughtered, she led a passionate campaign to save them. The story of her struggle is told in the children's book *Mustang: Wild Spirit of the West*, by Marguerite Henry.

Jack Kramer

Jack Kramer (1921–   ) is widely regarded as one of the top tennis players of the twentieth century. An aggressive player with a powerful serve, he won U.S. national championships in 1946 and 1947, the British Open in 1947, and four U.S. doubles championships during his career. Kramer was born in Las Vegas.

Paul Laxalt (1922–   ), who was born in Reno, was elected Nevada's governor in 1966. During his term, he helped transform the state's gambling industry by promoting legislation to allow businesses to invest in casinos. Laxalt was elected to the U.S. Senate in 1974. A close friend of President Ronald Reagan, he advised him during his 1976 and 1980 election campaigns.

Robert Laxalt (1923–   ) is a writer who brings to life the experience of Basque settlers in the American West. Laxalt grew up in Carson City and currently teaches at the University of Nevada in Reno. His best-known works include *Sweet Promised Land* and *The Basque Hotel.*

Greg LeMond (1961–   ), a champion cyclist, moved to Reno with his family when he was eight years old. He began winning bicycle races as a teenager, and he later moved to Europe to become a professional racer. In 1986, LeMond became the first American to win the Tour de France, the most famous bicycle race in the world. Shortly afterward, he was badly injured in a hunting accident, but he persevered and won the Tour de France twice more before retiring in 1994.

Liberace (1919–1987) was a pianist who became famous for his glittering costumes and flamboyant style. Wladziu Liberace learned piano when he was young and soloed with the Chicago Symphony in 1940. Through his television show in the 1950s he became a national celebrity. Liberace's act grew more popular—and more extravagant—with each passing decade. In the 1970s and 1980s he was a regular performer at the grandest of the Las Vegas hotels.

Liberace

Patrick McCarran (1871–1954), a native of Reno, served as a Nevada assemblyman and as a state supreme court justice before being elected to the U.S. Senate in 1932. During his 22-year stint in Congress, he worked hard to protect Nevada's economy, and as chairman of the Judiciary Committee, he played an important role in national politics. McCarran helped create the Federal Aviation Administration and was a sponsor of the Internal Security Act, which he believed would help protect the country against communism.

Lute Pease (1869–1963), who was born in Winnemucca, sought his fortune in ranching, mining, and hotel keeping before becoming a political cartoonist for the *Newark Evening News*. In 1949, Pease won a Pulitzer Prize for a cartoon about a coal strike started by the United Mine Workers Union.

Edna Purviance (1896–1958), a film star from the silent era, was born in Paradise Valley and grew up in Lovelock. While working in San Francisco, she caught the eye of actor and filmmaker Charlie Chaplin. Purviance got her first role in Chaplin's 1915 movie *A Night Out*. She then lit up the

screen in nearly forty more of his motion pictures, including such classics of the silent era as *The Champion*, *The Tramp*, and *Easy Street*.

Edna Purviance

Benjamin "Bugsy" Siegel (1906–1947) brought opulence to Las Vegas gambling. Siegel ran bootlegging, gambling, smuggling, blackmail, and murder-for-hire rackets in New York and California before realizing his dream of creating a gambling empire in the Nevada desert. In 1946 he built the Flamingo Hotel and Casino in Las Vegas, cheating his partners in the process. Six months later he was gunned down in his Beverly Hills home.

Benjamin "Bugsy" Siegel

George Wingfield (1876–1959) was a mining magnate who played a major role in Nevada politics during the early twentieth century. Wingfield owned twelve Nevada banks in the 1920s, and when they collapsed during the Great Depression, the state was almost ruined. He was widely recognized as the "boss" of the Nevada Republican Party from 1910 to 1932.

George Wingfield

Sarah Winnemucca (c. 1844–1891) was a Native American tribal leader, lecturer, and writer who sought greater justice for the Paiutes. Born in Humboldt Sink, she spent part of her childhood with a white family, and she later served as a scout and interpreter for the U.S. Army. After dishonest government agents caused members of her tribe to lose their land, she called attention to their plight in her book *Life among the Paiutes: Their Wrongs and Claims*.

Emma Wixom (1859–1940), a physician's daughter from Austin, became an internationally celebrated opera star. As a young girl, Emma was a naturally gifted singer who would spend hours in the open fields studying the songs of birds. After her first public concert in 1879, she performed across Europe and the United States under the stage name Emma Nevada.

Emma Wixom

Wovoka (c. 1856–1932), also known as Jack Wilson, was a Paiute mystic whose visions inspired a Native American religious revival known as the Ghost Dance movement near the end of the nineteenth century. Wovoka dreamed that the era of the white man was coming to an end and that the land would belong to the Indians once again. Wovoka's movement ended tragically when many of its followers were killed by U.S. troops at Wounded Knee, South Dakota.

Wovoka

TOUR THE STATE

Valley of Fire State Park (Overton) Weird rock formations shape the landscape of Nevada's largest state park. Some rock walls are covered with petroglyphs—drawings carved into the rock by Native Americans long ago.

Hoover Dam (Boulder City) Seven million tons of concrete went into the construction of this landmark, completed in 1936 to harness the power of the Colorado River.

Lake Tahoe State Park (Sand Harbor) Beautiful Lake Tahoe lies nestled in a valley of the Sierra Nevada. At Lake Tahoe State Park, you can camp along its shores.

Buckaroo Hall of Fame (Winnemucca) Stories and photographs, lariats and saddles, illustrate the lives of legendary local ranchers.

Ruby Mountains (Elko) Hiking, hunting, and camping are popular activities in this scenic region.

Imperial Palace Auto Museum (Las Vegas) More than 200 antique and custom cars are on display at this vast museum, including vehicles once owned by movie star Marilyn Monroe and singer Elvis Presley.

Southern Nevada Zoological-Botanical Park (Las Vegas) Animals and plants from near and far take center stage at Nevada's largest zoo.

Lied Discovery Children's Museum (Las Vegas) Visitors can learn about sound waves, monitor the weather, and even host their own radio shows at this interactive museum.

Great Basin National Park (Baker) Trails take hikers up Wheeler Peak, to the fascinating Lehman Caves, or through bristlecone pine forests with trees 3,000 years old.

Nevada Northern Railway Museum (Ely) At the former headquarters of the Nevada Northern, you can take a steam-powered locomotive past a ghost town or along a railway line made for hauling ore.

Liberace Museum (Las Vegas) Las Vegas performer Liberace was in love with glitter. Some of his most dazzling possessions are on display here, from a rhinestone-studded Mercedes Benz to a grand piano covered with mirrored tiles.

Nevada State Museum (Carson City) This museum in the former U.S. Mint boasts a working coin press, a woolly mammoth exhibit, and works by famed basket maker Dat-So-La-Lee.

Rhyolite In its heyday in the early 20th century, the gold mining town of Rhyolite had more than 50 saloons, three newspapers, and an opera house. Today it's a ghost town, and only a few desolate buildings remain, most famously the Bottle House which was constructed almost entirely out of empty bottles.

Lake Mead (Boulder City) This enormous reservoir was created when Hoover Dam was built in the 1930s. Nevadans flock to its cool waters to enjoy swimming, fishing, and boating.

Berlin-Ichthyosaur State Park (Gabbs) Visitors can explore the ruins of an abandoned silver-mining town at this state park.

Stewart Indian Museum (Carson City) Baskets, pottery, and other Native American artsare housed in the former Stewart Indian School.

Death Valley National Park (Beatty) One of the country's most dramatic landscapes, this valley of shifting sands lies in Nevada and California.

Lamoille Canyon (Elko) This dramatic gorge in the Ruby Mountains was formed by glaciers during the last ice age.

Lamoille Canyon

Northeastern Nevada Museum (Elko) Nevada history comes to life in exhibits on Native American culture, ranching and mining life, and the experience of the area's Basque settlers.

FUN FACTS

The longest Morse code message ever sent was the Nevada state constitution. It was transmitted from Carson City to Washington, D.C., in 1864.

Hoover Dam contains enough concrete to pave a two-lane highway from San Francisco, California, to New York, New York.

In 1999, Nevada had 205,726 slot machines, about one for every ten residents of the state.

The nation's only round courthouse is located in Pershing County, Nevada.

FIND OUT MORE

If you'd like to learn more about Nevada, look for the titles below in your library or bookstore. The websites listed at the end of this section offer information and links to other resources.

GENERAL STATE BOOKS

Fradin, Dennis B., and Judith B. Fradin. *Nevada*. Chicago: Children's Press, 1995.

Kummer, Patricia. *Nevada*. Mankato, MN: Capstone Press, 1998.

Stein, Conrad. *Nevada*. New York: Children's Press, 2000.

SPECIAL INTEREST BOOKS

Bouton, Kenneth, ed. *Nevada Trivia*. Nashville: Rutledge Hill Press, 1999.

Gibson, Karen Bush. *Nevada Facts and Symbols*. Mankato, MN: Hilltop Books, 2000.

Gutman, Bill. *Greg LeMond: Overcoming the Odds*. Austin, TX: Rainstree/ Steck-Vaughn, 1998.

Hacker, Shyrle Pedlar. *A Gold Miner's Daughter: Memoirs of a Mountain Childhood*. Boulder, CO: Johnson Books, 1996.

Knapp, Ron. *Andre Agassi: Star Tennis Player*. Springfield, NJ: Enslow Publishers, 1997.

Pioneer Stories of Nevada. Salt Lake City: Pioneer Publishing Co., 1996.

Stout, Carol Anne. *101 Things for Kids in Las Vegas*. Indianapolis, IN: 101 Things Inc., 1999.

FICTION

Moore, Ruth N. *Ghost Town Mystery*. New York: Herald Press, 1987. Teenage twins hunt for treasure in a Nevada ghost town.

Service, Pamela. *Vision Quest*. New York: Atheneum, 1989. A Native American artifact sends two Nevada teenagers on a mission into the past.

Snyder, Zilpha Keatley. *The Runaways*. New York: Delacorte, 1999. Three youngsters in a small town in 1950s Nevada fantasize about creating new lives by running away.

CD-ROMS

U.S. Geography: The West. Dallas: ZCI Publishing, 1994.

WEBSITES

www.state.nv.us Nevada's official state webpage, has a wealth of information about the state, and links to hundreds of more specialized pages.

www.nevadamagazine.com offers colorful feature articles.

INDEX

Page numbers for illustrations are in boldface.